T0163621

CASEWORKERS OR POLICE?

CASEWORKERS OR POLICE?

How Tenants See Public Housing

Alvin Rabushka
William G. Weissert

Hoover Institution Press
Stanford University • Stanford, California

HOOVER INSTITUTION PUBLICATION 186

For C.S.W. and Sol

CONTENTS

LIST OF TABLES

PREFACE

Public housing is grim and ugly; but so is most of the new architecture of the middle class, the stilt-houses and the ticky-tacky tracts. What effect does "grimness" or "monotony" actually have on the lives of people who live in ugly places? We have really no idea; . . . The controversial differences between the external appearances of public housing and middle-class housing are superficial. Substantial differences are in interior details which middle-class critics are never close enough to see. In the public housing projects of most cities, mothers sleep without fear of fire, and rats do not bite sleeping babies. These are concrete improvements in the life of disadvantaged people. These may conceivably outweigh the disadvantages of high-rise projects and excess bureaucracy—at least as compared to the alternatives available during the high days of public housing. Public housing has not worked magic. It has therefore been deserted intellectually by those who expect magic and by those who care less for the welfare of the inhabitants, about which little is known, than for the assumed social costs of bad urban planning. If public housing needs to be reformed—and it is certain that it does—*perhaps one step might be to ask tenants and potential tenants what should be done*. They are the ones who suffer personally, if anyone does.[1]

This book critically evaluates one low-rent public housing program in which both tenants and potential tenants were asked what should be done to improve the quality of life in public housing projects. In the fall of 1971, 72 Local Housing Authorities submitted proposals to the Department of Housing and Urban Development (HUD) for improving their housing management systems. HUD had invited these proposals as part of its Management Improvement Program (MIP) to upgrade the Authorities' management skills and cut operating costs.

The MIP added special funding to the normal operating budget of the Local Housing Authorities (LHAs) and thus financed an opportunity to institute changes in their management systems. Of critical importance was the stipulation that the management changes were to be planned and implemented with the participation of public housing residents. The MIP financed a three-year effort to achieve more efficient management coupled with improved resident services.

Thirteen large LHAs were selected from 72 applicants in June of 1972 to participate in the MIP. (A large LHA is one with 1,250 or more units under management.)[2] This book examines how one large housing authority—the Wilmington Housing Authority (WHA) in Delaware—utilized systematic information collected from its nearly 2,000 tenant families and elderly residents as a baseline for housing management decisions.

America's public housing program suffers a tarnished image. Both academics and administrators have, for their respective and often conflicting reasons, heaped abuse on the program. Many have, in place, put forth their own most-preferred, and presumably practicable, alternatives in pursuit of the goal of a "decent home" for every American. Too often these alternatives pursue the unrealistic or unattainable ideal of middle-class housing for all—unrealistic in that financial constraints are disregarded, impractical in terms of the steadfast opposition that public housing evokes in many communities.

This book takes a different direction. We seek no ultimate goals but ask instead how resources already invested or scheduled for investment in public housing can best be utilized. Over 3,000 LHAs shelter more than three million Americans and the federal government guarantees over $12 billion in tax-exempt LHA securities.

Over the three-year period that encompassed this study, plus a year of effort that led to its funding, a large number of people contributed their assistance. A list of key contributors includes Troy L. Chapman and Vince Lewis, successive Executive Directors of the WHA; Mary Kay Hitchner, Project Officer at the WHA; Dinah R. Griggsby, Deputy Director of Resident Services at the WHA; Cathleen Yordi, Kenneth R. Gervais, Jewell Shepperd, David North, Charles Nelson, Suzi Peters, and Colin Walters, all formerly of TransCentury Corporation; and Elinor Francis and Mazza Woldamosie of TransCentury Corporation.

Several persons, in particular, deserve a special note of thanks. Warren W. Wiggins, President of TransCentury Corporation, accepted our insistence that the MIP and its results were too important to file as just another unpublished government document and thus made possible the writing of this study for publication. A second individual who merits special consideration is Bruce Jacobs of the University of Rochester. His consulting efforts and comments on the manuscript were vital to its publication. Finally, we thank Hugh O. Nourse of the University of Missouri – St. Louis and several anonymous referees for their helpful comments on previous drafts of the manuscript.

Financial support for this study was embodied in the research and evaluation component of the HUD's MIP grant awarded to the WHA, and we thank HUD and WHA for the opportunity these funds permitted. Final work on the manuscript was completed at the Hoover Institution with support from the Domestic Studies Program. We thank anonymously the subjects of our study—the tenants of Wilmington public housing—and our teams of interviewers and part-time helpers. For editorial assistance we thank Barbara Roos. Finally, for assistance with typing we thank Claire Sundeen, Janice Brown, and Samirah Taha.

We graciously acknowledge the help of all the sources, who are not responsible for any errors the book may contain. Any errors of fact or interpretation must, in a co-authored project, be the fault of the other guy.

INTRODUCTION

Public housing has never been glamorous. When the program began in 1937 in order to supply temporary housing for middle class families badly hit by the depression and thus unable to afford private accommodation, its chief purpose was not really housing the dispossessed but rather to assist unemployed depression workers. As is true in the case of so many government programs, though, public housing outlived the depression, several wars, and even the postwar building boom. The last few decades have seen a steady change in the purpose and character of public housing: tenants' color has changed from white to black; tenants' families have grown larger, fatherless, poorer, and infrequently employed rather than temporarily unemployed. Public housing has also come to be the home of a growing segment of America's elderly population, the majority of whom are white. Public housing is now a fixture of American life, constitutes about 2 percent of the nation's entire housing stock, and represents a multibillion-dollar investment.

Despite this large and continuing investment, along with recent improvements in design, construction, and contracting for its development, the image of public housing has inexorably grown worse. By the late 1960s and early 1970s public housing had been designated as "housing of last resort," a place nobody would live unless they had no choice. Policy makers and scholars insisted that a *crisis* engulfed public housing. They entitled their essays in "crisis-ridden" language: "Is Public Housing Headed for a Fiscal Crisis?"[1] "Which of the Poor Shall Live in Public Housing?"[2] *Operating Costs in Public Housing: A Financial Crisis.*[3] *Politics and the Housing Crisis Since 1930.*[4] *Public Housing: The Politics of Poverty.*[5] Indeed, by 1973 the White House froze all new public housing construction as part of a suspension of all federally subsidized housing programs for low and moderate income groups, until a national policy review might recommend new and promising alternatives. Meanwhile, Lee Rainwater reported a bleak view of black family life in the federal slums of the St. Louis Housing Authority's Pruitt-Igoe project. Vandalism, rape, illegitimacy, school dropouts, job dropouts, and obscene behavior lurked *Behind Ghetto Walls.*[6] St. Louis took the message to heart and dynamited several of its buildings.

Now, in the mid-1970s, public housing is almost without any intellectual or political support either in the universities or in the policy-making corridors of Washington. Yet even as the image of public housing steadily deteriorates and its few remaining supporters speak in softer tones, tenants keep clamoring to get in.

Is it not ironical that people should want to move into this housing of last resort? And that people in public housing don't want to leave? Even some tenants who can afford better alternatives in the private housing market don't want to go. Every year public housing authorities have to evict people who exceed the income limitations of the program but who would stay if permitted. We have, in short, a paradox: nobody likes public housing except the people who live there and those who want to get in.

We stumbled across this paradox almost by accident. We set out in early 1973 to interview tenants about their problems, not to find out *if* they had problems. Since it was common knowledge that public housing tenants have problems, our task was to identify and count them in pursuit of a well-designed information and referral system. But to our surprise the tenants just would not own up to the problems we all knew they had. Moreover, the problems they had were not the ones we expected in view of the "crisis" literature on public housing.

We had anticipated problems with obtaining much "needed" social services, a crying need for day care, urgent needs for food, jobs, and money. We were sure the tenants would disdain their housing and be contemptuous of its management. We were certain they felt trapped in public housing and saw themselves as inadequate mothers, spouses, and so forth. We were expecting to reconfirm the presence of Rainwater's social pathology in our research environment. Because one study team member had interviewed in Watts after the 1964 riots, we rather incidentally also asked about crime and the police.

But only a handful of the almost 2,000 tenants we interviewed cited difficulties with obtaining social services. And they liked their housing. Despite a litany of potential ills ranging from defective screens to leaky roofs, most said their housing was adequate and rated the management in positive terms. Few felt trapped in public housing, and most tenants regarded themselves as effective and useful human beings, mothers, and spouses.

But they wanted police protection. More than anything else, they wanted security for themselves and their possessions.

These results did not fit the pathological world of Rainwater's federal slum. Months of data analysis, checking procedures, validating interviews, reanalyzing, and rechecking transpired before we finally discarded our preconceptions and the accompanying distasteful labels that sociologists had attached to public housing. This unhappy picture simply didn't fit the reality of the Wilmington Housing Authority. Moreover, what the tenants wanted was not an elaborate social services information and referral program; they wanted more security.

So the Wilmington Housing Authority set up a housing security force. When a panel of the same tenants was interviewed a year after the initial baseline set of interviews, it testified overwhelmingly in favor of the new security force. Though it had been in operation only a few months, a majority of respondents knew of the force and wanted it continued or expanded.

Because the survey data showed, convincingly, that almost nobody had problems obtaining needed social services, the management reduced by three-quarters the resident social services staff during the same period in which the security force was instituted. Satisfaction with social services did not decline with fewer available social workers; indeed, it increased.

We have lived with these data on the views and preferences of Wilmington's public housing tenants for more than three years. We have interviewed a sample of tenants in each of three succeeding years. And we have seen tenants corroborate the benefits of management decisions designed on the basis of tenant preferences. We have come to understand the views of these public housing tenants, that management's interventions based on these views can be both effective and well-supported, and that what has happened in Wilmington is not idiosyncratic but must be accounted for with a new paradigm on public housing.

Public housing tenants have been the recipients of housing policies that substitute middle class values of social scientists for first-hand knowledge of the clients of public housing. This book presents, in its place, an image of how tenants see public housing.

1

AN OVERVIEW OF PUBLIC HOUSING

Public housing statistics in the United States are very impressive in absolute terms even though proportionally fewer families and elderly persons live in low-rent public housing here than do their counterparts in Sweden, Britain, and the Netherlands. More than three million persons occupied just over one million public housing units as of 31 December 1974; the federal government spent $1.23 billion that year on direct provision of public housing services, not including the contributions of local governments.[1] From another perspective, the Department of Housing and Urban Development (HUD) estimates, on the basis of a sample of six cities, that the cost of providing a public housing unit in 1971 averaged $193 per month, of which the taxpayer contributed $137 per month.[2]

How is public housing construction financed? The United States Housing Act of 1937 provides that Local Housing Authorities (LHAs) may issue tax-exempt bonds to finance public housing. The act also guarantees these bond obligations through federal payment of an "annual contributions contract" to each LHA. HUD thus dispenses congressional appropriations to pay interest and amortization charges on public housing projects with the stipulation that community governments exempt these projects from local property taxes. In lieu of property taxes, up to 10 percent of rental collections may be paid to local government authorities.

The magnitude of this debt is impressive. As of 30 June 1974, $12.7 billion in federally guaranteed, tax-exempt LHA securities were outstanding. In 1974 alone, nearly $1 billion in bonds were issued.[3] The public housing program thus shelters millions of people and costs billions of dollars.

The United States Housing Act of 1937 put the public housing program on a permanent legal basis, but as Table 1 shows, its subsequent expansion has been uneven. In 1950, only about 200,000 units were under management in the 1,077 projects that existed. Since then, the rate of expansion has mirrored the ups and downs of the national economy. It played second fiddle to the Korean War effort and suffered severely in the minirecession of 1958. In particular, the Eisenhower administration (1953 – 1960) revealed little enthusiasm for the program, and the quantitative goals embodied in the 1949 Housing Act were attained in but the barest fraction. Still, the total number of projects had tripled and the number of units more than doubled by 1960; the next decade witnessed a similar rate of expansion—by 1970 over 9,000 projects contained nearly 1.25 million units in all stages of management and preparation.[4] The most dramatic expansion took place in the early Nixon years, directly following the passage of the United States Housing Act of 1968; close to one-third of the total stock of public housing dates from the 1968 legislation. Public housing genuinely flourished under President Nixon, perhaps despite his political beliefs and wishes, until he suspended the operation of all principal federally subsidized low and moderate income housing programs in early 1973 pending a complete review and evaluation.

Passage of Public Law 93-383, the Housing and Community Development Act of 1974, on 22 August 1974, ended the freeze on new public housing construction. It authorized the Secretary of HUD to specifically earmark at least $150 million for the development or acquisition of *new* low-income housing after July 1974; an additional $15 million was earmarked for Indians and Alaskan natives. Public Law 94-116, passed on 17 October 1975, specifies a further $50 million for new low-income housing, and the 1976 Housing Authorization Act requires HUD to use $85 million for new public housing construction in fiscal year 1977. These sums pale in comparison with pre-1973 spending, however; new authority to construct is now only a token gesture toward the program.

How is public housing managed? Although the federal government funds LHA debt payments in the form of an annual contributions

TABLE 1

LOW-RENT PUBLIC HOUSING: YEARLY TREND IN CONTRACT AND
CONSTRUCTION ACTIVITIES, 1950-1974

	Active Housing Units		
Calendar Year	Placed Under Annual Contribution Contract	Placed Under Construction or Rehabilitation	Made Available for Occupancy
1950	74,248	31,642	270
1951	88,929	69,224	9,994
1952	41,513	55,514	58,258
1953	10,406	31,785	58,384
1954	–	16,244	44,293
1955	29,965	8,568	20,899
1956	43,097	4,916	11,993
1957	5,391	20,850	10,513
1958	24,293	22,602	15,472
1959	29,770	15,824	21,939
1960	11,437	29,209	16,401
1961	27,867	30,493	20,965
1962	25,094	22,402	28,682
1963	36,031	24,030	27,327
1964	37,429	25,591	24,488
1965	26,281	33,298	30,769
1966	43,514	31,999	31,483
1967	70,277	34,015	39,021
1968	77,801	71,606	72,638
1969	108,783	64,231	78,003
1970	101,932	104,410	73,723
1971	58,228	72,230	91,539
1972	80,319	44,760	58,590
1973	33,453	27,807	52,791
1974	22,438	19,050	43,928
TOTAL	1,112,496	912,300	942,363

SOURCE: *1974 HUD Statistical Yearbook* (Washington, D.C.: U.S. Government Printing Office), p. 104.

contract, local agencies bear the responsibility for developing and operating public housing. They legally own and operate public housing within a municipality, county, several counties, or a group of cities, and remain legally distinct from local governments to avoid limitations on bonded indebtedness. Each is administered by a permanent staff that is responsible to a board of commissioners. The authorities select sites, plan, develop, and manage projects, and set rents, income limits, and other eligibility requirements.[5] As of 31 December 1974, some 3,079 LHAs administered 10,748 projects, encompassing a total of 1,316,126 housing units, under annual contributions contracts with the federal government.[6] Nearly half of the LHAs are located in the southeastern and south central sections of the nation,[7] areas in which public housing does not suffer a tarnished image.

What are the distribution and size of the units managed by LHAs? At the end of 1972, 49 percent of the agencies managed fewer than 100 units, whereas only 13 percent supervised 500 or more. As expected, then, the majority of housing programs were located in small communities, but Table 2 shows that 42 percent of all housing units were in cities of 250,000 and over. The 140 largest LHAs managed over 60 percent of all public housing units, with the New York City and Chicago agencies alone responsible for about 12 percent.[8] Nearly half of all public housing was thus in large projects in Chicago or New York or small projects in small or medium-sized southern cities and towns.

Statutory requirements constrain the selection of tenants for admission to public housing. Each LHA sets maximum income limits. The rule is that the tenant's maximum income, at the time of admission, may not be more than five times the rental charged for private unassisted standard housing, which is taken to be the community's typical low-cost private rental housing for blue-collar workers. These eligibility maximums ranged in 1971 from a high of $7,800 for a four-person household in New York to $4,700 in San Antonio, which reflect geographical differences in housing costs.[9] Many housing authorities evict the tenants whose incomes exceed, on any annual recertification, the admission maximums by more than 25 percent.

Local agencies also set public housing rents, again on the basis of local area rent levels. Rents charged for public housing units must be at least 20 percent less then decent, unassisted private housing rentals. Thus, a 20 percent gap exists, in principle, between the lowest income at which the individual can rent decent private housing and the highest

TABLE 2

PERCENTAGE OF HOUSING PROGRAMS AND UNITS REPRESENTED BY LHA
PROGRAMS, BY 1970 POPULATION OF PLACE, AS OF 31 DECEMBER 1974

Population Size Group	Percentage of LHAs	Percentage of Units	Distribution of Population Inside SMSAs[a]
Under 2,500	35	5	8
2,500–9,999	32	10	15
10,000–49,999	24	19	27
50,000–99,999	5	11	12
100,000–249,999	3	13	10
250,000–499,999	1	13	7
500,000–999,999	b	13	9
1,000,000 and over	b	16	13

SOURCE: Derived from *1974 HUD Statistical Yearbook* (Washington, D.C.: U.S. Government Printing Office), p. 108.
[a]Standard Metropolitan Statistical Areas.
[b]Less than 0.5 percent.

income level at which the individual is eligible for public housing, since tenants who can afford private housing (whose income is 25 percent above the admission upper limit) must be evicted. Naturally, public housing is minimally a 20 percent bargain for its occupants compared with the cost of comparable private rental units, since the LHA, by statute, must charge 20 percent less. Finally, congressional legislation in 1969, 1970, and 1971 legally bound rents to a maximum of 25 percent of tenant income, with federal subsidies to make up the difference in lost rental income to local agencies; these comprise section 213(a) of the Housing and Urban Development Act of 1969, better known as the Brooke amendments, named for their chief supporter, Senator Brooke of Massachusetts.

Although public housing thus confers substantial financial benefits on its tenants, the proportion of eligible families who live in public housing is small. Muth cites an analysis of public housing which estimates that only 7 percent of the eligible population actually lived in public housing units in 1960. Despite perhaps a doubling since 1960, the percentage is still small.[10] That public housing is in great demand is confirmed in the long waiting lists for admission.[11]

A National Housing Policy Review report, completed during the 1973 freeze on federal housing subsidies, calculates that the benefits of public housing are greatest for tenants whose annual incomes range between $1,000 and $5,000: for these families, the mean annual benefit is estimated at about $1,000.[12] The $3,000 (median) annual income of families in public housing is much less than the $10,000 annual median income of all American families in 1971. The public housing subsidy enables the recipient to live in standard rather than substandard housing. Since only a small proportion of eligible persons actually reside in public housing, however, the subsidy is distributed unevenly. Table 3 shows that in 1972 approximately 50 percent of the families in public housing had annual incomes over $3,000, while 95 percent of all families in the United States with annual incomes under $3,000 were not served by the program.

What kinds of people have lived in public housing? During its first two decades, the occupants comprised a heterogeneous mix of veterans, elderly, upwardly mobile low-income families, temporarily unemployed families, and a small minority of publicly assisted poor. In recent years,

TABLE 3

DISTRIBUTION OF LOW-RENT PUBLIC HOUSING BY INCOME CLASS, AS OF 31 DECEMBER 1972

Gross Income	Total Households	Households Served by Public Housing	Public Housing Households as Percentage of All Households
$0 – 999	1,800,000	25,910	1.5%
1,000 – 1,999	3,800,000	283,120	7.4
2,000 – 2,999	4,300,000	248,520	5.8
3,000 – 3,999	4,000,000	183,860	4.7
4,000 – 4,999	3,800,000	124,290	3.2
5,000 – 5,999	3,800,000	73,260	2.0
6,000 – 6,999	3,600,000	45,760	1.3
7,000 – 7,999	3,800,000	27,900	0.7
8,000 or more	39,600,000	42,420	0.1
TOTAL	68,500,000	1,055,050	1.5%

SOURCE: *Housing in the Seventies* (Washington, D.C.: Government Printing Office, 1974), page 128.

this heterogeneity has given way to a growing proportion of elderly persons and broken families with welfare-dependent mothers and children. Today's tenant is poorer than he or she was in 1960. Between 1960 and 1972, the median income of all American families rose 90 percent, while the median income of public housing families rose only 21 percent.

This comparison should come as no great surprise. Tenants with rising incomes either voluntarily seek better private housing or face possible eviction when income exceeds statutory limits. As a result, the proportion of families receiving welfare assistance and/or benefits rose from 35 to 71 percent during this twelve-year period; the elderly population rose sharply from 13 to 41 percent; and the proportion of minority group members, chiefly blacks, rose to 60 percent.[13] Table 4 summarizes the characteristics of present tenants.

The income and rental limits that apply to black and poor welfare tenants in the face of accelerating costs, especially maintenance, force LHAs to seek larger federal operating subsidies or face possible bankruptcy. One political response has been to designate units for the elderly. It is cheaper to house the elderly because they require smaller units and thus produce a higher density and greater rent return per square foot of building space. The elderly are also typically less destructive of property, and thus their units require lower maintenance than those of larger, younger families.[14]

Legislative History of Public Housing[15]

Legislation affecting tenement housing in New York City originated in 1864. Its stated purpose was to remedy overcrowding and unsanitary conditions in privately owned housing; it was also the keystone of future legislation for programs intended to house the poor. Large-scale public housing became national policy, however, only after passage of the Wagner-Steagall Act of 1937, also known as the United States Housing Act of 1937.

An earlier limited government investment in public housing did not meet with any meaningful measure of success. World War I witnessed a small-scale program of public housing for defense workers that concluded, at war's end, with losses in the millions. Public housing subsequently stagnated throughout the 1920s and was not reborn until the

TABLE 4

RACE AND OTHER CHARACTERISTICS OF PUBLIC HOUSING FAMILIES, BY AGE OF HEAD OF FAMILY, 1970

Characteristic	Family Head Under 65		Family Head 65 or Older	
	White	Nonwhite	White	Nonwhite
Median income (dollars)				
All	3,479	3,425	1,767	1,792
No earners	2,457	2,466	1,693	1,609
One earner	4,540	4,437	3,406	3,361
Two or more earners	7,788	7,703	7,673	6,956
Racial composition within age group (percentage)				
Reexamined for continued occupancy	25.7	74.3	62.2	37.8
Newly admitted	37.1	62.9	72.5	27.5
Labor force status (percentage)				
No earners	39.5	39.0	89.8	77.4
One earner	54.4	54.6	9.6	20.4
Two or more earners	6.1	6.4	0.6	2.2
Income from public sources (percentage)				
None	51.9	47.1	3.4	7.5
Public assistance	35.9	46.1	30.9	51.6
Social security or other transfers but no public assistance	12.2	6.8	65.7	40.9
Family size (percentage)				
One person	8	4	68	53
Two persons	18	14	25	26
Three or four persons	39	36	5	13
Five or more persons	36	46	2	8

SOURCE: Adapted from Henry J. Aaron, *Shelter and Subsidies: Who Benefits from Federal Housing Policies?* (Washington, D.C.: Brookings Institution, 1972), p. 117.

TABLE 5

LOW-RENT PUBLIC HOUSING UNITS DESIGNED FOR THE ELDERLY, 1960–1974

Year	Number of Units[a]
1960	25,241
1965	121,757
1966	160,689
1967	196,160
1968	239,326
1969	286,910
1970	301,172
1971	316,829
1974	338,429

SOURCES: *1971 HUD Statistical Yearbook* (Washington, D.C.: U.S. Government Printing Office), p. 153; and *1974 HUD Statistical Yearbook* (Washington, D.C.: U.S. Government Printing Office), p. 11.
[a]The number of units refers to all stages of reservation, construction, and management.

National Industrial Recovery Act of 1933 empowered the President to create an emergency Public Works Administration (PWA). The PWA administrator, in turn, promptly established a Housing Division in June 1933 that could, among its activities, buy or build its own housing projects. Employment for workers in the building and heavy-industry trades was the chief objective of the Housing Division.

PWA's public housing construction program was short-lived. A federal district court held in 1935 that the federal government could not use its power of eminent domain to acquire property on which to construct public housing for the purpose of selling or leasing it to private citizens; this purpose was not, the court ruled, a proper use of eminent domain. State courts, however, differed in their interpretation: the New York Court of Appeals held that state use of eminent domain for purposes of slum clearance was lawful. Although the federal government could not build or own public housing, it could finance state and local ownership if the states would pass the appropriate enabling legislation upon enactment of the Wagner Housing Act of 1937. Greater local involvement in public housing construction and operation thus replaced the prior centralized structure of public housing development.

Public housing in the United States is, with the full set of subsequent amendments, shaped by the Housing Act of 1937. Only financial support was centralized in federal hands, with states and communities reserving the right to participate. LHAs, not the federal government, would undertake to build and manage public housing. The following list features some provisions of the 1937 Housing Act:

1. A permanent Housing Authority was established under the Department of the Interior.
2. The building of public housing was to be tied to slum clearance.
3. Rents were to be charged against tenant income levels, thus creating eligibility criteria.
4. Local tax exemptions were required for federally assisted public housing.

We should not retrospectively view the Housing Act of 1937 as a high-priority assault for housing the persons we now label the "dependent poor." Indeed, had not the depression left a large segment of the middle class in a temporary condition of poverty, the act might not have passed at all. These persons were, after all, only a temporarily submerged middle class who would, with but a little assistance, shortly rise to reclaim their position. Public housing was not charity nor were its tenants to be given free housing. Project rents had to be sufficient to pay all operating costs—maintenance, administration, and payments in lieu of local government taxes. The rent requirement, in effect, stipulated that the unemployed and paupers were not welcome in public housing.[16]

World War II overshadowed development of the public housing program until it could be re-debated in the mid- to late-1940s and culminate in the 1949 Taft-Ellender Act. But a booming private sector, generating jobs and housing in the suburbs, downgraded congressional conviction that public housing was an important national need or issue in the postwar period. Many tenants left public housing as their incomes rose above maximum limits. The submerged middle class had risen and moved out: the dependent poor and southern blacks had begun to move in.

A chief provision of the 1949 act was the authorization of 810,000 units by 1955. Production quotas were stymied, however, by the Korean War and an unsupportive Eisenhower administration. Public housing also became increasingly linked to slum clearance and urban renewal. New public housing barely kept pace with, and in many places even fell behind, urban renewal-induced destruction of low-income housing.

Some of the inner-city poor displaced by urban renewal were relocated into public housing. Public housing construction was increasingly confined to poor inner-city locations, and its tenants came increasingly from bulldozed urban renewal areas. Since public housing was from 1954 "open" or integrated, site selection for new projects stirred up volatile political opposition in each community. The requirement of local approval, a feature in the original 1937 Housing Act, obstructed the dispersal of new units as each neighborhood vociferously opposed public housing. The fear of integration increasingly made site selection infeasible except in slum areas.

Significant legislative changes appeared with the 1959 housing legislation. Priority was given to elderly persons over 65, and single persons were declared eligible for public housing. A subsidy payment of up to $120 per unit occupied by senior citizens encouraged LHAs to favor the development of projects to house the elderly. Political support for housing white, elderly, and "middle-class-in-behavior" poor people is, of course, much easier to secure than support for housing minorities prone to destructive and violent behavior. It is possible to imagine one's parents living comfortably in public housing and to support public spending for that end; it is easy to be unsympathetic to the "undeserving poor."

Housing legislation in 1959 further decentralized the administration of public housing. Local authorities were given more flexibility in determining income limits and setting rents for public housing tenants. And in the following year, the previously restrictive policy of not providing welfare and social services to tenants was reversed, thus increasing the incentives to local authorities to accept greater numbers of welfare recipients. Apart from an increase in both rent subsidies and construction cost limitations for elderly housing, the 1961 legislation did little more than authorize the expenditure of funds remaining from the 1949 act—the permission to build almost 100,000 new units.

The Department of Housing and Urban Development (HUD) was created in the Housing and Urban Development Act of 1965. Its chief innovative features affecting public housing concentrated in the area of more efficient construction, the "turnkey" method in which private builders are awarded contracts for completed projects, and in the management of leased private housing for public housing tenants. Still the bulk of public housing tenants live in project sites, not in scattered-site or private leased housing.

Passage of the Brooke amendments in 1969, 1970, and 1971 is a watershed in the legal evolution of public housing. The amendments, whose financial consequences we shortly explore, set public housing rental ceilings at 25 percent of a tenant's income, thus reducing rental revenues to the LHAs. Federal compensation was intended to replace lost revenues arising from reduced rentals, but it fell short of these losses and gave rise to a near bankrupt state of public housing operation for many public housing agencies. The Housing and Community Development Act of 1974 was written to help alleviate this condition.

What, if anything, is significantly new or innovative in the 1974 legislation? First, a chunk of new moneys allocated to finance development or acquisition of public housing units is earmarked for members of any Indian tribe or Alaskan natives. Second, to assure sound management practices in the operation of public housing projects, the secretary of HUD may prescribe the following requirements:

1. Selection of tenant families with a broad range of incomes to avoid concentrations of low-income and deprived families with serious social problems.
2. Establishment of procedures to assure prompt payment of rent and prompt processing of evictions in the case of nonpayment.
3. Establishment of tenant-management relationships to assure satisfactory standards of tenant security and proper enforcement of standards of maintenance.

Third, the Secretary of HUD is authorized to supply up to $500 million in annual contributions for operating costs—this to diffuse the fiscal crisis in public housing.

No specific number of units is designated as a new production target; rather, limits to the cost of annual contribution contracts restrict the extent of new construction. Public housing has emerged neither as a dramatic winner or loser in the 1974 act. The program will be maintained much as before with provision for an operating costs subsidy. What is new is the legislative intent to reopen public housing to a broader range of income groups whose monthly rent payments could permit public housing to operate on a more viable financial basis. And the legislation has a law-and-order ring to it, which correctly reflects, we believe, the preferences of public housing tenants.

Public Housing in Wilmington

The Wilmington Housing Authority (WHA) was established in 1938 and opened its initial stock of 200 dwelling units for occupancy in 1943. The housing stock under the WHA's jurisdiction had grown to 1,980 units in early 1971, which constituted nearly 8 percent of Wilmington's housing supply. Of these, there were 516 units for the elderly; 1,200 units in family projects; 211 completed units of scattered-site housing; and 44 units of leased housing located throughout the city and county. An additional 774 units were either being developed or planned. Projects for families consist largely of two-story brick rowhouses and range in size from one- to four-bedroom units. Projects for the elderly consist overwhelmingly of high-rise buildings that contain efficiency and one-bedroom units; only a handful are in garden-type apartments. Despite a modernization program that put them in fairly good shape, family units have required an abnormally high volume of maintenance. High-rise projects for the elderly are in excellent shape and provide an extremely attractive environment for their tenants.

WHA's operations are concentrated in the City of Wilmington, although it can also legally operate in portions of New Castle County. WHA has, until recently, implemented urban renewal plans with a gross cost in excess of $40 million since 1951, and it has also assumed responsibility for housing-related components of Wilmington's Model Cities program in 1970.

Demographic changes in New Castle County typify the shifting population composition in metropolitan areas throughout America. The proportion of New Castle County's population that lives in the city of Wilmington dropped from 51 percent in 1950 to about 21 percent in 1970. During this 20-year period, the population in Wilmington declined in absolute numbers from 110,356 to 80,356; New Castle County, conversely, grew from 108,523 to 385,856 (excluding the city of Wilmington). These migration patterns altered the racial composition in Wilmington: the nonwhite population increased from 16 to 44 percent by 1970.[17]

Wilmington is still highly segregated on a residential basis. Concentrations of nonwhite residents range from as low as 0.5 percent in some areas to as high as 93 percent in others. Most of WHA's family tenant projects are located in the chiefly nonwhite residential districts.

Approximately half of Wilmington's 28,000 housing units are owner-occupied, with the remainder renter-occupied. Although nonwhites make up 44 percent of Wilmington's residents, they own about 16 percent of the total housing units and therefore rely chiefly on the rental market for accommodations. Much of this rental housing is old, in need of rehabilitation, and overcrowded. Pre-1900 construction is located in predominantly nonwhite areas.

This generally old and run-down housing that constitutes a large chunk of the private rental market for nonwhite, low-income families stands in sharp contrast to the more attractive post-World War II garden apartments that comprise the bulk of WHA's family project units. Moreover, the rapid inflationary increase in housing costs further accentuates the difference between the quality of housing in WHA and what tenant monthly rentals could purchase in the private market. There is, in short, no present substitute for the low-income families now living in public housing, except to suffer a precipitous decline in their consumption of housing, or face dramatically higher housing costs, if forced out onto the private housing market.

2

THE CRISIS IN
PUBLIC HOUSING

The crisis in public housing is twofold. One dimension is the real and intensifying fiscal crisis that confronts the nation's LHAs; the other dimension is intellectual. Indeed, the intellectual crisis has probably contributed, in recent years, to the fiscal crisis, as the government has reduced authorizations and appropriations for public housing construction, impounded funds appropriated to pay deficits in operating costs, and in 1973 froze new public housing construction altogether. Critics are not confined to one small field but represent the thinking and writing of experts in sociology, economics, and political science. Sociologists have published perhaps the most dramatic research on public housing, economists the most quantitative, and political scientists the most polemic-ridden.

The Intellectual Crisis

Sociological Analysis and Public Housing

Sociological analysis points to the "culture of poverty" as a chief cause of failure in public housing.[1] Lee Rainwater's analysis of the Pruitt and Igoe Housing Projects in St. Louis is the classic case of large-scale overconcentration of poverty and total failure. Completed in 1955 and 1956, the projects were among the first high-rise public housing developments in the city. They were the first and only St. Louis Housing Projects to each exceed 1,000 units and consisted, in all, of 43 buildings on 57 acres near the city's central business district. Despite a general nationwide shortage of public housing units for eligible families, the vacancy rate in St. Louis projects was 13 percent by 1967.[2] Indeed, by 1970 the projects were perceived as being so crime-ridden and physically deteriorated that the St. Louis Housing Authority closed down 26 of its high-rise buildings and concluded that it could no longer keep up with maintenance and repairs.[3]

What is the culture of poverty and why must it lead to public housing failure? Rainwater offers the following pathology:

High rates of school dropouts.
Poor school accomplishment for those who do stay in.
Difficulties in establishing stable work habits on the part of those who get jobs.
High rates of dropping out of the labor force.
Apathy and passive resistance in contacts with people who are "trying to help" (social workers, teachers, etc.).
Hostility and distrust toward neighbors.
Poor consumer skills—carelessness or ignorance in the use of money.
High rates of mental illness.
Marital disruptions and female-headed homes.
Illegitimacy.
Child abuse or indifference to children's welfare.
Property and personal crimes.
Dope addiction, alcoholism.
Destructiveness and carelessness toward property, one's own and other people's.[4]

Overconcentration of the lower class elements in high-rise public housing breeds an environment in which any individual is very likely to become involved in or be a victim of violent behavior. Poverty and destructiveness are, for Rainwater, the two cardinal characteristics of lower class life: how can public housing succeed in these circumstances? Successful public housing is possible, in this view, only if the poor are disentangled from their culture of poverty. But the exact same words could be written about the poor who live in private housing in neighborhoods whose residents consist solely of lower class blacks. This pathology of the "culture of poverty" makes it difficult for any housing to be successful, i.e., to provide well-maintained housing at reasonable rentals the poor can afford. But large concentrations of high-rise public housing projects are simply more visible to the public at large than scattered private rental accommodation, however badly deteriorated, and thus are easier to criticize.

Vandalism and crime are the alleged culprits of Pruitt-Igoe's demise in St. Louis; overconcentration of female-headed families, blacks, un-skilled laborers, and welfare recipients is, in turn, the culprit of van-dalism and crime. A shift in the composition of public housing tenants from the "working poor" to the "dependent poor" thus lies at the heart of failure in public housing.

To be fair, Rainwater's report is not so much an assault on public housing as it is a complaint about the distribution of income in America, which he claims impels the worst-off into a life style of violence, crime, and destructiveness. We should not construe the behavior of low-income blacks *Behind Ghetto Walls* as an indictment of federal policy in the field of public housing provision. Rainwater's subtitle, *Black Family Life in a Federal Slum,* has made it difficult to disentangle his analysis of poor black people from an implicit condemnation of public housing. These two become synonymous among the public at large. Indeed, the opponents of public housing are able to argue, with some persuasiveness, that public housing is itself a cause of this violent behavior, the resolution of which is not Rainwater's suggested redistribution of income but instead the dynamiting of Pruitt-Igoe—despite the fact that most of Rainwater's subjects said they liked their housing apartments very much and 80 percent said it was better than their previous dwellings.[5]

Political scientist Eugene J. Meehan has recently reexamined and documented in extraordinary detail the experience of the St. Louis Housing Authority.[6] He affixes blame for its difficulties, especially in the Pruitt and Igoe projects, on a coupling of statutory and financial de-velopments with destructive tenant behavior, the last of which reinforces the Rainwater "culture of poverty" pathology. Meehan first charges that the design, bidding, and construction of the high-cost Pruitt and Igoe projects, devoid of even the minimal housing amenities provided in the wartime projects completed in 1942, was a case of straightforward robbery by the local construction industry. To worsen matters, the shoddily designed and constructed units were not very durable and neces-sitated excessive maintenance expenditures.[7] Second, Meehan lists the federal measures that eroded the financial soundness of the Authority. Income limits for tenants, which engendered a poor community of residents, combined with rentals limited to 25 percent of these low incomes (the Brooke amendments), constrained the rent-taking capacity of the Authority. Regulations also limited the accumulation of financial reserves to a maximum of 50 percent of one year's rentals, a policy which undercut the increased maintenance needs that accompany the physical aging of projects. Third, Meehan repeatedly quantifies how vandalism and crime helped bring about the demise of Pruitt-Igoe. In 1965, for example, more than 20 panes of glass were broken each day.[8] Vandalism costs increased by 5 percent each year since 1965 and consumed by 1969 about 40 percent of all maintenance labor costs and 30 percent of all the materials used in maintenance—slightly more than $2 million in the five-year period ending in 1969. "In 1969 alone, Pruitt consumed some 7,000 light bulbs, 16,000 window shades, and 20,000 panes of glass; it absorbed the services of an 84-man crew, at a cost of half a million dollars, . . ."[9]

But Meehan's own explanation of this destructive tenant behavior rings of the "culture of poverty" thesis. He links the many apparently illegitimate children of Aid to Dependent Children (ADC) families with project debilitation and vandalism, crime gang activity, and general disorder, "particularly in view of the serious lack of educational facilities, entertainment, or recreation in the project areas."[10] "Unemployment was particularly marked among the young and the black and was very probably associated with the sharp increase in crime and vandalism that plagued the projects toward the end of the 1950s."[11] At the same time, Meehan castigates the St. Louis Housing Authority's establishment of a costly Division of Human Resources in 1963 to supply social services to these deprived tenants.[12] He calls this and other social programs a phony public relations effort.[13]

Meehan also charges that overcrowding, the cramming of nine to ten persons in a poorly ventilated, 900-square-feet unit of living space, caused or contributed to undesirable social implications.[14] In Hong Kong, though, the density in public housing is four- to fivefold that of Pruitt-Igoe. At a rate of 24 square feet per adult, a family of five lives in one room consisting of 120 square feet in an equally hot and humid climate, and this extreme density produces no serious destructive tenant behavior.[15] Despite the failures in Pruitt-Igoe, Meehan still notes that conditions in public housing were superior to those from which some tenants moved prior to entering the projects.[16]

Meehan's solution to the failure of conventional public housing in St. Louis is to change congressionally imposed fiscal policies and also develop more adequate managerial control over the operation of the housing program, which would result in stronger federal control over local operations.[17] Nowhere does Meehan suggest how to cut down the vandalism and destructive tenant behavior in the search of fiscal solvency—save to ameliorate, by implication, the contributing social conditions, that is, to attack the "culture of poverty."

Roger Starr's analysis of the New York City Housing Authority addresses the shift in composition of tenants to the dependent poor.[18] Why are New York City's housing projects viable? Why do more people want to get into them than are willing to move out? Starr attributes success to the fact that the city's public housing is acceptable to the working poor; in other cities, by contrast, public housing is disproportionately the home of the *nonworking, dependent poor.* Since, according to Starr, the stock of low-rent private housing in New York is no worse than in other large cities and since the architectural design of New York public housing is no better, successful administration in New York thus belies the high-rise thesis of public housing failure. High-rise *per se* is not a necessary or sufficient cause of public housing failure. According to Starr, the true threat lies in the attributes of the dependent poor. If the working poor flee public housing because of high rates of crime and vandalism associated with the dependent poor, deterioration would also threaten heretofore viable housing projects in New York.

When is public housing viable? For Starr, only when the majority of tenants consist of male-headed households, the elderly (who were once a part of the work force), and households headed by disabled or unemployed males who possess working-class characteristics. It is not viable, he concludes, when the majority of tenants consist of female-headed households who are unemployed and are supported chiefly by ADC. These women, largely black, possess few skills, low motivation, and are marked as being outside the working class.

Starr believes that different attitudes toward work and life between the working and dependent poor are crucial to the success of a public housing program. He attributes the chief source of crime and vandalism to fatherless households. It is the activities of alcoholics, junkies, and young delinquents—mostly members of ADC families—who disrupt and disfigure life and property in public housing.

We might note one response to Pruitt-Igoe in the Housing and Urban Development Act of 1968: Congress restricted the construction of high-rise elevator buildings for public housing families. But Starr puts the blame squarely on the tenants, not on the structures in which they live.

We accept neither proposition. This book about tenant preferences and behavior in Wilmington challenges the sociological norm: public housing has been a viable housing subsidy program for lower income families in Wilmington with (96 percent) black, unemployed, welfare-dependent, poorly educated, fatherless households.

Economic Analysis and Public Housing

Public housing is in high demand, as the long waiting lists attest, because tenants clearly achieve a higher level of well-being than in private housing. High demand reflects low-rent housing or better quality housing at the same rent.[19] For the 163,235 public housing families who moved in between October 1973 and September 1974 (about 483,000 persons in all), mean gross rent was $52.76; new elderly tenants averaged $46.91. Median income of the tenants moving in was $3,171, virtually identical to the $3,142 figure of existing families.[20] These figures are the facts of public housing life and explain its popularity among tenants and potential tenants.

Economists couch their analysis of public housing in the complementary criteria of efficiency and equity. Observing that a public housing unit represents up to a $1,000 annual subsidy for tenant families with incomes between $1,000 and $5,000, they see in the same glance that 95 percent of all families in the United States with annual incomes under $3,000 receive no direct benefits from the program. This distribution of benefits is uneven and thus inequitable. Some economists argue that rent supplements would be less costly yet supply equivalent housing benefits; if so, public housing subsidies are inefficient. Equity and efficiency are interrelated: every dollar spent on public housing is one less dollar available for other forms of housing assistance; every dollar concentrated on substantial help for a small group of the poor means that fewer dollars are available for spreading the benefits further.

We might begin by setting public housing expenditures in the context of overall federal housing subsidies and tax policies. The estimated cost to the treasury of allowing homeowner deductions for mortgage interest and real estate taxes in 1973 was, as Table 6 shows, $7.9 billion. Households with incomes over $7,000 enjoyed 90 percent of the tax breaks; those with incomes under $3,000 enjoyed less than 1 percent. Of course, homeowners are treated no differently in this regard than are owners of rental housing or other income-producing assets, who may lawfully deduct interest and tax costs of doing business from their returns. What is different and especially beneficial to homeowners is that the implicit rental income of owner-occupants is not taxed (nor of any owner-used consumer-durable). The loss to the treasury from not taxing the implicit net rental income, over and above expenses, is not a subsidy to homeowners (though many call it so) but is nonetheless an unevenly distributed tax benefit. The higher the implicit net rental income of a home and the higher the tax bracket of the taxpayer, the greater the benefit to the owner-occupant. By comparison, direct budget outlays for subsidized housing programs totaled $1.8 billion in fiscal year 1974.[21] Of these outlays, less than one-quarter of subsidized new housing units constitute public housing units. Downs concludes from his study of federal housing programs that "the present federal housing subsidy structure as a whole does not focus its benefits mainly upon low-income households, but provides even more complete coverage of middle- and upper-income households (especially since a high proportion of the latter are homeowner occupants)."[22]

How does the public housing program stand up under his scrutiny? It is, he concludes, a sound instrument for satisfactorily housing low-income households with no major social problems, but the destructive behavior of some poverty households distorts its effectiveness.

Are there any workable solutions to this seemingly intractable problem? Downs suggests that public housing accommodate a wider range of income groups that can afford rents which cover operating costs; nor should the practice continue of evicting households whose incomes rise above stated limits. How to attract these higher-income families into public housing is not spelled out. Although Downs favors a large-scale demonstration program of housing allowances, he does not believe that "a modern industrialized society can totally eliminate the need for publicly owned and operated housing for certain large-sized groups unable to obtain decent quality housing in private markets."[23]

Henry J. Aaron of the Brookings Institution has also investigated the benefits that federal housing policies confer on different segments of the

TABLE 6

ESTIMATED REVENUE COST OF ALLOWING HOMEOWNERS DEDUCTIONS FOR MORTGAGE INTEREST AND REAL ESTATE TAXES, 1973

Adjusted Gross Income Class	Returns with Mortgage Interest and Real Estate Tax Deductions				
	Number of Returns (thousands)	Percentage of all Returns	Total Cost of Deductions (millions)	Average Cost of Deduction	Cost Deductions as Percentage of Tax Liability
Under $3,000	112	0.6	$2.6	$23	1.1
$3,000–$5,000	490	5.3	31.2	64	1.8
$5,000–$7,000	1,436	16.0	130.6	91	3.2
$7,000–$10,000	4,000	33.1	538.8	135	5.7
$10,000–$15,000	7,360	46.4	1,307.9	178	6.3
$15,000–$20,000	5,688	65.8	1,675.3	295	9.0
$20,000–$50,000	5,690	78.6	3,274.3	581	10.6
$50,000–$100,000	479	86.2	693.8	1,448	7.0
$100,000 or more	118	88.7	289.0	2,449	3.1
TOTAL	25,326	31.6	7,943.6	314	7.6

SOURCE: *Sixth Annual Report on National Housing Goals.* Message from the President of the United States, 94th Congress, 1st Session, House Document No. 94–18, 14 January 1975 (Washington, D.C.: U.S. Government Printing Office, 1975), p. 18.

population. In particular, he challenges public housing on grounds of equity: "A number of issues concerning public housing remain unsettled. The most important is the fairness of giving a sizable subsidy—$800 per year on the average—to a small fraction of low income households and nothing to most of the rest."[24]

Other investigators suggest that a basic problem is simply lack of funds. For instance, Robert Brown's study of public housing in Pittsburgh, published in 1959, pinpoints the lack of dollars as a chief obstacle to an adequate supply of public housing.[25] He proposed, in place of this expensive subsidy of a few, a rent-subsidy program with broader coverage.

Richard Muth is critical of public housing on grounds of both efficiency and equity.[26] He notes, first, that tax resources invested in public housing are inefficient because public housing is too often built on very expensive cleared slum land; this feature raises the capital costs of public housing construction.[27] Second, the present program provides a small fraction of eligible families with more housing than they would otherwise consume—this is because tenants place less value on public housing than the true cost of the subsidy. Third, the Davis-Bacon Act stipulates that federally assisted or financed projects are subject to minimum wage rates set by the Department of Labor—no contractor who wins a public housing construction contract may pay less than these rates. Thus, construction costs of public housing projects are frequently higher than if the identical project were built privately. For these three reasons, public housing is inefficient and wastes a portion of the tax money. On the basis of prior analysis that related income increases to a decline in the proportion of substandard housing, using census figures for 1950 and 1960, Muth projects that an income subsidy equal to the market value of the increased housing provided by public housing would reduce total occupancy in substandard housing far more than just for the small segment of families now enjoying the public housing subsidies.

How would this work? If the additional $130 spent on housing each month for the 7 percent of lower income families who live in public housing were divided among all eligible families, $9.10 each month could be given to all eligible families. From his prior regression analysis, Muth projects that this sum could eliminate as much substandard housing as the present lottery-type public housing system and simultaneously avoid the inequity of allocating scarce public housing units to only a small fraction of eligible households. Moreover, a rent certificate

program would allow individual consumers, who have detailed knowledge of their own situations, to make their own housing decisions. One
can question the assumptions and analyses that underpin Muth's projec-
tions of the decline in substandard housing that an extra $9.10 each
month would produce, since they rest upon a 1960 data base. There is no
question, though, of his correctness in saying that 85 percent or more of
all eligible low-income families receive no benefits from the program.
His critique on criteria of efficiency and equity cannot be faulted on
either logical or empirical grounds. But these critiques provide no
solution to the current problems of public housing operation and the
preservation of the stock of public housing, unless Muth is prepared to
contemplate abandonment or sale of these projects. Of course the
political question is: will Congress vote the necessary equivalent income
subsidies to permit the tenants to maintain their current housing quality
and well-being, and can HUD process these for the one million families
now in public housing, as the projects are abandoned?

Heilbrun echoes the inequitable character of public housing subsidies
when he confirms that the stock of public housing relative to the large
number of eligible households is inadequate. "Instead of providing
uniform benefits to all who qualify, the program provides costly benefits to a few and nothing for the rest. (By way of analogy, imagine that free
public elementary education were available only to a small proportion of
families and that pupils were selected from long waiting lists.)"[28]

The National Housing Policy Review report, *Housing in the Seventies*,
computes both the efficiency and equity of all federally subsidized
housing programs.[29] Efficiency is the relationship of benefits to costs. If
the benefits exceed or equal costs, the program is efficient; if costs
exceed benefits, it is inefficient. Any assessment of housing subsidy
costs must include not only the federal government's direct subsidy
payment but also all other costs incurred in the program, such as
administrative costs, foregone taxes, default costs, and special interest
rate subsidies. The report enumerates and then tries to compute the
following efficiency measures:

1. Production efficiency—the ratio at which government transforms
   tax dollars into extra housing.
2. Construction efficiency—the relationship between the development
   costs of a project built conventionally and an identical project built
   through government subsidy programs.
3. Transfer efficiency—the ratio of the cash grant supplied in the

housing subsidy to the market value of the subsidy (the value to the tenant can be measured by the size of the unrestricted cash grant that he would accept in lieu of the subsidy).

4. Program efficiency—ratio of the increase in the occupant's welfare measured in terms of an unrestricted cash grant to the total costs incurred by government to achieve that increase in welfare.

Efficiency, as the foregoing discussion demonstrates, goes hand in hand with equity. The benefit of a housing subsidy program is judged not only by the costs it entails but also by the extent to which it channels assistance to low-income families in need. An equitable program is one that serves a majority of low-income recipients.

How has public housing fared against these twin criteria of efficiency and equity? The report estimates a technical ratio of .85. This means that public housing authorities spend $1.17 to produce $1.00 worth of housing. In actual dollar terms, the estimated $184 monthly expenditure per unit of public housing yields a unit with a market value of only $157. Technical inefficiency accounts for $27 of this sum. Moreover, in addition to the cost of managing the housing, the cost of administering the public housing program runs another $9 per month (e.g., checking the eligibility of applicants).

How do the other efficiency measures turn out? Production efficiency yields a ratio of .74 and transfer efficiency, .75. The latter figure means that for each $100 monthly installment that the government spends on public housing, tenants place a personal value of $75 on the housing subsidy.

We have previously noted that 95 percent of all families with annual incomes under $3,000 are not served by public housing; thus the benefits are confined to a relatively small segment of the target population.

We now summarize the report's major findings on public housing subsidies.

1. Families served by public housing are usually poorer than those not served; however, most of the families in the lowest income groups are not served.
2. The overwhelming majority of public housing tenants occupy better housing and are able to purchase more of other nonhousing goods than they would in the absence of the program.
3. Taxpayers incurred an average annual cost of $1,650 per household in public housing.
4. Because resource costs to produce public housing are greater than

those required to produce comparable conventional housing and
because tenants place a lower value on the transfer-in-kind than a
cash grant, tenant welfare is increased by about $0.50 for every
dollar spent.

Although public housing vastly improves the quality of housing that
tenants consume and is thus a success in the eyes of this minority of
low-income families, the fact is that the overwhelming majority of
eligible families remain unserved. This troubles the economist.

Robert Weaver's remarks on the economists' obsession with equity
provide an appropriate means for concluding this section.

> Once there is abandonment of the fetish of absolute equity within eligi-
> ble income groups which has dominated much of the recent discussion of
> housing subsidies, it is possible to approach these issues rationally.
> Obviously there must be concern for many objectives, including efficiency,
> social aims, and reasonable equity. . . . Equity is a parallel concern. But
> it is only one of many—not always the paramount one and certainly not
> the only one.[30]

Weaver questions, from preliminary assessment of HUD's housing
allowance experiments, the proposition that a demand-oriented subsidy
of the rent certificate type can completely and effectively replace all
production-oriented subsidies.

Emphatic talk of equity and efficiency obscures one important current
issue—how best to supply housing services to the tenants now living in
the existing stock of public housing until—or better yet, if—some
alternative programs find them substitute housing. Snail-paced implementation of the current substitute—the Section 8 leased housing
program contained in the 1974 Housing and Community Development
Act—suggests that the nation's one million public housing units will
house over three million persons for some time to come. How best to
continue this provision is not found in the crisis literature of economics.

Political Analysis and Public Housing

To sample political science analysis of low-rent public housing is to
reveal a polemic-laden literature. The central claim of these critics is that
the government has reneged on its promise to supply a "decent home"
for every American as explicitly stated in the 1949 Housing Act. One
explanation of this unmet promise is found in the work of Lawrence

Friedman. In *Government and Slum Housing: A Century of Frustration* he traces from the late nineteenth century the history of legislation designed to eradicate slums and substandard housing.[31] Despite the fact that the program provides a significant supply of decent homes for poverty-level people, the full promise in the program never materialized. Why? Simply because the poor are a minority of Americans and possess little bargaining power in American politics. They have been unable to overcome the obstacles of race and income segregation, two powerful villains in housing history.

Leonard Freedman's examination of the controversy over public housing addresses the legislative process in which the politics of public housing is debated and the interest groups that support or oppose public housing.[32] He singles out as villains a select set of powerful opposition groups whose economic interests lie in the building, selling, or financing of housing: the National Association of Real Estate Boards, the National Association of Home Builders, the United States Savings and Loan League, the Realtors' Washington Committee, and local affiliates of these associations in communities where public housing was proposed. Freedman's analysis purported to show that the enemies of public housing were more effective than its proponents. They wielded greater resources in money and personnel and repeatedly found allies in Congress who often opposed public housing on ideological grounds.

His historical recounting of the waxing and waning of support for public housing from Roosevelt through Johnson is elaborated in far greater detail in Nathaniel Keith's *Politics and the Housing Crisis Since 1930*.[33] Keith painstakingly adumbrates the blow-by-blow account of the political forces that have forged the nation's housing policies since the mid-1930s and how they have opposed and inhibited the facilitation of that policy. His central thesis is "that it is the alignment of political forces, not the availability of material and financial resources, which has primarily determined the rate of progress over the past 40 years, or lack of progress, in housing in the United States. . . ."[34] In particular, although liberals in both parties have largely enacted major housing and community development legislation, conservatives have clustered in the appropriations committees of the two houses of Congress where control over the purse strings has throttled the broader legislative mandates. The belief that middle America does not like its "undeserving poor," especially as a neighbor in public housing, obstructs widespread implementation of the program. For Keith this is an inherently incurable element in the nation's legislative philosophy. Although small efforts to subsidize housing for low-income families will remain a feature of public life, the prospects for a dramatic expansion in federally subsidized low-income housing are not encouraging.

Effective utilization of existing public housing and the operating subsidies it receives is, we believe, the most fruitful topic that research into public housing can address. The realities dictate neither a closing down of existing programs, its immediate or even near-term replacement by some new program, nor a dramatic expansion of subsidized housing for every low-income family. The principal object of this book then, in light of the foregoing, is to tackle head on the issue of effective management in the present public housing program.

The Housing and Community Development Act of 1974 temporarily forestalls, at least on paper, the growing crises in public housing. Chief among these is the fiscal crisis: revenues have not kept pace with operating costs. Although inflation has been the most recent and newsworthy culprit, the fiscal crisis had been foreseen since the late 1960s. Despite the alleged presence of numerous failures in the public housing program, it nonetheless fills a void for those who cannot afford the increasingly expensive alternative of private housing. For persons presently served by public housing—who cannot afford to pay dramatically higher rents—to live within their means requires some resolution to the problem of ever-rising operating costs in LHAs.

The Financial Crisis

Construction and management of low-rent public housing is the province of LHAs, not of the federal government. Federal assistance for public housing is provided in the form of an Annual Contributions Contract between the LHA and HUD. This contract supplies the funds to service the debt on monies that local authorities must borrow to develop and construct housing stock. In practice, before construction begins, HUD enters into an annual contributions contract, not to exceed 40 years, which covers interest and amortization on long-term bonds issued by the LHA. These bonds are exempt from federal income taxes, which makes interest rates lower than on other taxable federal securities; they are, as well, backed up by the full faith and credit of the United States government and thus constitute a near risk-free investment.

A second form of federal financial assistance consists of subsidy payments made to local authorities on behalf of certain groups of persons whose resources preclude payment of normal public housing rentals: the elderly, the disabled, the handicapped, displaced families from urban renewal, and unusually large and poor families. Local financial assistance takes the form of exemption from local property taxes; local governments take up to 10 percent of rental collections in lieu of charging local property taxes. Ten percent of rental collections is lower than a fully assessed local property tax on LHA buildings.

Until 1969, the operating costs of public housing were met from rents and utility charges collected from tenants; indeed, LHAs were required to remit any excess of revenue over current operating expenses to the federal government. In the early postwar years, a large proportion of the annual contributions contract was offset by these remissions, which have virtually disappeared in the 1970s.[35] Many LHAs had even accumulated reserves, up to the allowable maximum of half of one year's rentals, to tide them over in periods of revenue shortfalls. But by 1969, the viability of LHAs was seriously under challenge.

In 1969 Albert Walsh published an essay in the *Journal of Housing* entitled "Is Public Housing Headed for a Fiscal Crisis?"[36] Although the system of pegging rents to cover all costs save those of debt service had worked during the first three decades of public housing, Walsh now suggested that the terms *low cost* and *low rent* were no longer interchangeable, that, in fact, the inflationary spiral of operating costs now increasingly outdistanced the rents that public housing tenants could afford to pay. Additional income produced by rent increases had not kept pace with routine operating expenses. In New York City, for instance, the LHA had already resorted to withdrawing reserves to cover operating deficits; future withdrawals threatened, Walsh argued, the very solvency of the LHA. One cure lay in increased subsidies from HUD.

In the same year, Frank de Leeuw published an Urban Institute study entitled *Operating Costs in Public Housing: A Financial Crisis*,[37] in which he explored the reasons that public housing rental income had been running well below operating costs for LHAs in 23 large cities. De Leeuw's central finding was that price and wage inflation are the major causes of increased operating costs, accounting for some 80 percent of the rise in costs between 1965 and 1968. Other factors include aging of the public housing stock and the large number of minors per dwelling unit. Although LHAs calculate rentals on a cost-per-unit basis, de Leeuw found that rent increases had been running consistently 25 percent behind cost increases.

De Leeuw suggested three possible policies to relieve the financial crisis. The first and most obvious is a rent increase—a policy that would, in an inflationary situation, soon place an extremely heavy burden on the poorest tenants. A second policy entails discriminatory tenant selection against large families that inflict high maintenance costs on the LHA and in favor of, say, the elderly. His third suggestion was that the federal government increase its statutory payments or supplemental payments to avoid increasing the rent burden on tenants. This could be done, for example, if the size of the subsidy were tied to general price and wage increases beyond control of LHAs.

The changing pattern of occupancy to the lowest-income families and the incidence of rising costs due to inflation had already generated a fiscal crisis by 1969. But the loss of revenue due to the 1969, 1970, and 1971 Brooke amendments greatly intensified the crisis. The Brooke amendments, beginning in 1969, further reduced LHA revenues by stipulating a rent-to-income ceiling of 25 percent for each tenant. Brooke II, in 1970, further liberalized the definition of income deduction, and Brooke III, in 1971, set a complete application of the 25 percent ceiling rent-to-income payment to tenants receiving public assistance.[38] This last amendment alone resulted in a loss of about $77 million in rental revenues that previously came from public welfare agencies. Many tenants subsisting on welfare had their relief checks trimmed by the amount of their rent reductions. The effect was to transfer much of the cost of housing relief families from local welfare departments to LHAs.

To compensate for rent losses mandated under the Brooke amendments, Congress authorized HUD officials to subsidize operating costs but, perhaps influenced by the "crisis" exposes of public housing, did not appropriate sufficient funds to cover the entire revenue loss. The formula used to determine the extent of this operating cost subsidy is tied to the fiscal year 1972 expense level of each LHA, with subsequent increases of 3, 3, 5.5, and 5.5 percent in the four succeeding fiscal years.[39] Actual costs, though, have risen more rapidly than this, and LHAs have correspondingly reduced operating services and deferred maintenance, which has in turn necessitated a costly modernization program introduced by HUD in the mid-1970s.

Rental ceilings in the face of escalating operating expenses are a major element in the financial crisis of public housing. Mean monthly rent as of

30 June 1974 was $45.27; corresponding monthly operating expense, however, was $73.18.[40] This difference, in the main, represents the $25.42 monthly unit operating subsidy appropriated by Congress.

It is informative to look at the expense reports of LHAs. Most dramatic is the high cost of repairs and maintenance: ordinary monthly maintenance costs $22.87 and extraordinary maintenance an additional $1.76. In absolute terms, local agencies spent $287 million, an expense about equal to 55 percent of rental collections. Furthermore, the LHAs, not the tenants, pay utility charges which average $19.52 per month, or about $288 million in the fiscal year ending 30 June 1974. Unless tenants can be induced to reduce utility consumption and inflict less wear and tear on their housing units, the rental ceilings foreshadow an unending dependence on the annual operating costs subsidy.

Approximately $170 million was provided in operating subsidies for fiscal year 1973, but this amount was insufficient to compensate for revenue losses mandated under the Brooke amendments. Congressional persuasion forced the Office of Management and Budget to release another $100 million that had been impounded, thus increasing the operating cost subsidy for fiscal 1973 to $270 million. The Housing and Community Development Act of 1974 incorporates operating costs subsidies as a permanent feature of the federal government's annual contributions to LHAs; it authorizes, all told, up to $500 million in fiscal year 1974 and $560 million in fiscal 1975. Thus the financial crisis in operating costs has been temporarily forestalled, presuming HUD pays these subsidies promptly.

Research Procedures

The Management Improvement Program (MIP) was an ambitious effort, with special HUD funds, to facilitate more cost-effective provision of public housing services. It included a structural reorganization of the Wilmington Housing Authority (WHA), development of a fully automated management information system, and establishment of a tenant social services referral system. Most important for this book was the development of a diagnostic social survey and information system for WHA tenants.

The survey of tenants was predicated on several objectives. First, it would provide basic information to WHA management, to social service workers, and to tenants themselves. The WHA might make more effective demands upon federal, state, city, and county social service programs on the basis of systematic and quantified information on tenant "needs" as revealed by the survey; and management could more effectively respond to the preferences of tenants for proposed changes in the housing environment and in the WHA's operations.

A set of anticipated findings was taken for granted. On the basis of social science and social work literature and just plain good sense, WHA staff expected vocal criticism of its operations. They also anticipated uncovering widespread concern over family and neighborhood problems. Finally, they naturally assumed that tenants wanted but lacked extensive social services. Surely tenants would be in great need of these services. The survey would inventory them and refer needy families to available services. Where gaps existed, new services could be added.

But common sense turned out to be wrong. Anticipated demand for social services did not materialize. Indeed, the rationale for maintaining the WHA's existing social services staff was undermined.

Where did these expectations of unmet social service needs go wrong? At the time of the MIP application, WHA possessed little systematic knowledge of tenant preferences or their needs. The management had estimated that most tenants received some sort of public assistance and knew that three-quarters of these obtained ADC. They also knew that 80 percent of tenant families were female-headed households. Wilmington tenants, on paper, resembled those of Pruitt-Igoe: over 96 percent of these low-income, fatherless households were black. Would they not be in substantial need?

Public housing, along with other nonhousing social services, presumably serves the purpose of helping poor people who need better housing, transportation, health, education, and other middle-class amenities. Indeed, the very concept of "helping" the poor, the elderly, or the minority group member, i.e., providing more services and opportunities for them, implies that their present consumption falls short of some appropriate social level. No reasonable person could argue that poor persons prefer their culture of poverty to that of middle-class America. It seems fair to say that research about and programs designed on behalf of the poor are predicated upon a set of values that asserts the social desirability to convert the poor, so far as resources permit, into middle-class citizens, either through an increase in their income or the increased provision of special services.

Although the 1973 baseline survey of all WHA residents was predicated upon the existence of widespread tenant needs, a set of contrary findings forced a reconceptualization of the "needs of the poor." It became necessary to distinguish between the social service experts who attributed a set of needs to the poor and the needs the poor themselves perceived. By extension, it became necessary to distinguish between activities that poor tenants perceive as desirable and activities that social service agencies and their staff perceive as desirable. In practice, this entails keeping middle-class values separate from an understanding of poor tenants. We found valuable conceptual clarification in the notion of "rational man," a concept we borrowed from economic theory.[41]

The notion of rational man can be construed as a summary statement of human nature that reads as follows: people act in their own self-interest. Although self-interest is often equated with wealth-maximizing behavior or pecuniary motives, it is not exclusively synonymous with the single-minded pursuit of money. Some people maximize nonpecuniary goals, e.g., philanthropy. To say that people act in their own self-interest is simply to say that individuals are able to rank their preferences from most-preferred to least-preferred and can select the option highest on their list. This is what the economist means when he says that people are maximizers of utility—they select the available option that provides them with the greatest satisfaction. To analyze human behavior, economists ask about the self-interest of the relevant participants to any action.

For us, the critical aspect of this conception of rational man is that each individual defines his own self-interest *subjectively*. This implies, of course, that individuals have and can express preferences. Moreover, subjectivity implies that there are no such things as correct preferences. This point is crucial and cannot be overemphasized. What may be a correct preference for one person may be anathema to another. Preferences are personal valuations based on whatever principles, values, and tastes an individual may hold, however acquired. There is no such thing as an objectively correct preference except from each individual's own point of view. To say that an individual is able to order his preferences correctly is not to say he has the "truth" for others.

This concept of man leads directly to the following question: how do the poor maximize utility? Or, in laymen's words, what gives the poor satisfaction? What do they want? It is logically incorrect to ask: what do they need? The concept of need denies the subjective nature of individual preference. From the standpoint of middle-class America the poor public housing tenants may *need* a considerable increase in the provision of certain goods and services. The poor from their own standpoint, however, may not consider these items necessary or desirable. Therefore, we do not and cannot hold up any arbitrary standards against which we can measure the physical, social, or psychological *needs* of the poor, save those put forth by the poor themselves.

To cite a major finding, by way of anticipation, the survey revealed that only a very small percentage of poor tenants encountered difficulty with obtaining needed social services. An overriding concern, instead, was for greater protection of person and property. Law and order, not more social workers, ranks first in the tenants' preference structure.

We have already seen another illustration of the "rationality" of tenants in the long waiting lists for admission to public housing. Tenants are economically rational in the sense that public housing is preferred, at the present price, to the higher-cost private market alternative rentals. Poor, fatherless households are no different in this regard than the middle class, that is, in choosing the least costly among comparable quality units.

The MIP thus allowed WHA to adjust its policies to conform with tenant preferences, not with their "presumed needs." From the standpoint of the subjectivity of preference, poor public housing tenants are identical with persons of all income classes who make choices and seek satisfaction from them. The chief difference is one of financial constraint: they cannot afford to buy a middle-class standard of living. But the preferences poor tenants set forth are as valid as those of higher-income Americans and can play a significant part in helping insure efficient utilization of the resources invested in public housing.[42]

The Surveys

Two sets of surveys were an inherent part of the MIP: one set entailed interviews with family tenants, elderly tenants, and a random sample of persons drawn from the WHA's waiting list; another set focused on the 47 social service agencies in the Wilmington area that could service the WHA's tenants.

In addition to the initial diagnostic survey of all public housing tenants, which would help inform subsequent management decisions, a program of annual reinterviews in the succeeding two years was drawn up that would elicit the tenants' assessment of any forthcoming management changes in program or policy. The initial survey conducted in early 1973 included the following:

1. All heads of household in the family projects (1,240 families).
2. All elderly residents (711 tenants).
3. A sample of persons on the WHA's waiting list (126 persons).

Public housing tenants were used as interviewers with the stipulation that they interviewed only in projects other than those in which they lived; family housing tenants interviewed other family tenants, and elderly tenants interviewed other elderly tenants. Quality control staff in TransCentury Corporation, which bore overall responsibility for the survey, randomly checked on 20 percent of the respondents. This initial round of surveys was designated as Wave I in the projected longitudinal analysis.

Findings from Wave I appear in Chapter 3, and shifts in management policy, in response to these baseline data, are discussed in Chapter 4. We should reiterate that a primary objective of the MIP was to incorporate tenant preferences in WHA decisions and to document subsequent changes in tenant attitudes. Thus an appropriate sample plan for the Wave II reinterview of family and elderly tenants to be undertaken in January 1974 was drawn up as follows:

The sample frame utilized for the family tenants consisted of the 1,119 family tenants who were interviewed the previous January and were still living in WHA housing in August 1973. (Since the completion of Wave I, 121 tenants had vacated their units.) To insure that each tenant interviewed in Wave I possessed an equal probability of appearing in Wave II, a proportional stratified simple random sample was drawn from the remaining 1,119 tenants. Tenants were first stratified by project site and then randomly sampled within each project site. Table 7 displays by project site the distribution of those interviewed in Wave II. This sample frame yields percentages for the family tenant sample that fall within 4.4 percent of their true value at the 95 percent confidence level—that is, Wave II results vary within 4.4 percent of those that a reinterview of the entire set of 1,119 tenants would obtain. This sample frame balances considerations of cost and accuracy.

To demonstrate accuracy of selection, we compare respondents' characteristics in Wave II with those of persons not interviewed in Wave II. Table 8 reveals that the two groups do not differ significantly in any way; we can thus make inferences from the Wave II sample to the entire family tenant population with a high level of confidence.

TABLE 7

BREAKDOWN OF FAMILY SAMPLE BY PROJECT SITE

Project	Tenant Information System Code	Number in Sample Frame	Number Interviewed	Percentage of Tenants Interviewed (Sampling Fraction)
Eastlake	1	125	38	30.4
Southbridge	2	140	42	30.0
Eastlake Extension	3	121	34	28.1
Southbridge Extension	4	127	37	30.2
Riverside	5	302	85	28.2
Scattered site	8	120	35	30.2
Asbury Manor	12	44	12	27.3
Evans, Kennedy	13	22	7	31.9
Scattered site, Madison Garden	15	118	36	30.6
TOTAL		1,119	325	29.0

TABLE 8

COMPARISON OF SAMPLED WITH OTHER FAMILY TENANTS, BY PERCENTAGES

Characteristic	In Wave II (n=325)	Other Tenants (n=793)
Female head of house	86.2	83.9
Head of household less than 36 years old	48.8	51.6
Tenant employed	28.5	31.4
Seeking employment	73.8	72.6
In WHA less than three years	40.8	41.1
Reported as victims of crime	26.1	23.7
Income below 50 percent of poverty line	35.6	35.6
Average family size (number of persons)	4.2	4.2

Wave II reinterviews with elderly tenants rest on a different frame. Wave I vividly documents that elderly tenants are neither dissatisfied with management of the WHA's elderly housing units nor suffer any significant degree of personal problems or difficulties in obtaining needed social services. Based on the consistency of these findings with results reported in other similar studies, it was possible to keep within budget constraints and reinterview a substantially smaller proportion of elderly tenants in Wave II. A total of 90 elderly tenants were listed through simple random selection independent of project site—an over-sample drawn to assure the completion of 75 successful reinterviews.

Wave III interviews, completed during January 1975, were restricted to family tenants. (The stable set of attitudes and perceptions that were revealed in the Wave II survey of elderly tenants reinforced Wave I findings of strong support for WHA management, virtually complete satisfaction with housing conditions, and an almost total absence of social service problems.) Wave III plays an important role in the final evaluation of the three-year experimental MIP. Significant shifts in policy had taken place in direct response to Waves I and II; Wave III provides tenant evaluation of these important changes. Every effort was therefore made to reinterview each of the 325 family heads tapped in Wave II who still lived in WHA housing—the number of successful reinterviews was 294. As before, WHA tenants conducted these interviews, and TransCentury undertook quality control measures.

Rarely do social scientists encounter an opportunity to undertake longitudinal assessment of ongoing policies and garner subjects' views on policies that have been altered in light of their previous responses. The three-year MIP conducted in Wilmington provides one of those rare opportunities. It is encouraging to learn that policies can be designed on the basis of tenant preferences and can be modified, extended, or discontinued on that same basis, even if the tenants live in a "culture of poverty." Lawrence Friedman suggested that "one step might be to ask tenants and potential tenants what should be done." This book offers the promise that resources allocated to public housing can be more effectively utilized if managers possess systematic information about tenant preferences.

A second set of surveys was conducted with the 47 principal social service agencies operating in the Wilmington area. Information about each was collected on: whom to contact, eligibility, fees, days and hours of operation, and delays between the application for services and delivery. These organizations covered a wide variety of programs: emergency services, medical service assistance in the home, transportation, counseling and referrals, community organization and advocacy, adoptions, foster and day care, residential and day camps, preschool education, recreation, room rentals, and credit unions. The survey also sought to ascertain if the agencies shared their resources and data with each other. On the basis of these surveys, a directory of social services handbook was compiled and distributed to all tenants. The intent was to make more readily available the services that tenants could successfully utilize through a systematic social service referral system.

3

THE TENANT'S VIEW
OF PUBLIC HOUSING

An image of "housing of last resort" tarnishes public housing. From the standpoint of the middle-class home owner or the critical intellectual, public housing is a disgrace. But this point of view is grounded in the preferences of people who do not live in public housing nor who necessarily asked public housing tenants for their own opinions. What is the tenant's side of the story? Is it one of the stereotypical multiproblem family that needs extensive social services and close supervision? Do tenants feel trapped in public housing? Is public housing as bad as the critics allege? Answers to these and other questions asked of public housing tenants erase much of its tarnished image.

Two major themes structure the format of this chapter. The first set of results bears upon the tenant's perception of life in public housing and his relationships with housing authority management and field staff. A second set examines general issues of social services, or what is more commonly termed *basic human needs*. Here the issue is poverty, not one of public housing.

Who is the typical tenant? First, he or she is extremely stable in terms of mobility. More than 96 percent of the family tenants had lived in Wilmington for the past three years; less than 0.5 percent had lived there less than one year. Corresponding percentages for the elderly and waiting list respondents were 98 and 93.

Second, the typical tenant lives below the recognized poverty level. Mean reported family income is $3,500 and the median income is just over $3,000. More than 70 percent of tenant families received some welfare assistance in the past year with 77 percent also receiving surplus food.

The typical family tenant is poor and dependent on welfare. He or she is also unemployed, black, and poorly educated. About 84 percent of heads of household are women, and less than one-third have a high school diploma. Less than one family in five has two parents living in the unit. This is indeed the sociological model of a modern public housing tenant, the allegedly intractable tenant with whom housing authorities must cope.

Elderly tenants display a somewhat different racial mix. Excluding Compton Towers (180 units) and 1802 West Street (13 units), both of which are chiefly black, the remaining fraction of the 711 elderly residents is 85 percent white. In aggregate terms, 60 percent of the elderly tenants are white, and 40 percent are black. The high-rise projects tend either to be disproportionately black or white, rather than integrated on any proportional formula basis.

An Evaluation of Public Housing

Wave I sought responses to three substantive aspects of tenant life in public housing: (1) a general perspective of life in public housing, (2) an evaluation of management performance, and (3) satisfaction or dissatisfaction with the housing unit itself.

The overwhelming majority of tenants in family project sites do not project the tarnished image that middle-class critics inflict on public housing. Only 26 percent say they feel trapped in public housing. Fewer than half of those respondents, 12 percent, are ashamed of living in public housing.

And the elderly? One general pattern emerged that persisted throughout the entire baseline survey: elderly residents invariably put forth more favorable perceptions of public housing and its management than did the tenant families. This result came as no surprise in light of previous research on the urban elderly poor.[1] High-rise units for the elderly are modern, clean, well-maintained, and constitute an attractive environment for elderly individuals and couples. There is no question that Wilmington's high-rise elderly public housing units are totally successful in terms of its residents' evaluation. Less than one in twenty feel trapped in public housing; one in forty is ashamed to be there; and only 12 of 711 respondents report difficulties obtaining credit because of his or her address. This is hardly a negative image![2]

Are the physical units themselves livable? Table 9 displays the percentage of residents who report no specific problems with the units and the environment in which they reside. Elderly tenants are virtually without complaints on every dimension and, with the exception of noise level, more than 60 percent of tenant family heads report no problems on any dimension of livability.

TABLE 9

PERCENTAGE OF TENANTS REPORTING NO PROBLEMS OF LIVABILITY IN PUBLIC HOUSING

Item	(n=1,240) Families	(n=711) Elderly
Appearance	66.8	95.8
Noise level	57.9	93.2
Size of equipment	61.1	96.5
Living space	62.4	93.2
Electrical outlets	72.2	98.0
Appliances	73.9	98.5
Plumbing	63.4	96.8

The family tenants who express concern with the appearance, noise level, plumbing, etc., of the units are less critical of the immediate neighborhood environment. Less than 30 percent find the neighborhood unattractive and only one in seven believe the area is overcrowded and thus not a decent place to live. Only one in six considers the apartment building itself unsatisfactory. Compared with the disquieting sociological analyses of other municipal public housing projects, Wilmington's tenants project a favorable image.

A second aspect of tenant life bears upon individual contacts and perceptions of the WHA's management and, in particular, tenant evaluation of each project site's resident manager. Tenants were asked if they had any problems with the WHA's management on a broad variety of topics: rent collection, assignment of dwelling units, strictness of rules, racist attitudes, collection of back rent, the position of the resident manager, and indifference toward tenants. Table 10 sets forth the percentages of family and elderly tenants who report *no problems* with WHA in each of these policies or activities. Note, once again, that the elderly are virtually without complaint. And, on the average, about three-quarters of family household heads report little difficulty with the way in which the WHA operates or carries out its responsibilities. It is especially encouraging to find that racism is the least cited problem in the eyes of family tenants, of whom 98 percent are black.

TABLE 10

PERCENTAGE OF TENANTS REPORTING NO PROBLEMS WITH WHA MANAGEMENT

Do you have problems with WHA management because of	(n=1,240) Families	(n=711) Elderly
The way it matches tenants with apartments	71.0	94.5
The way it collects rent	73.7	97.2
The way it collects back rent after increases due to recertification	69.9	95.2
The position it gives the resident manager	80.1	99.2
Its rules being too strict	75.2	98.2
Its lack of care about tenants	62.0	96.2
Its racist attitudes	83.0	97.5

The WHA's central office is located in downtown Wilmington, quite some distance from many of the actual project sites. Tenants thus have little reason or opportunity to deal directly with central office staff. Of far greater prominence is the site's resident manager, with whom tenants have frequent contact. Indeed, we shall argue in the next chapter that the resident manager plays a crucial role in the effective delivery of housing services; for now it suffices to demonstrate that in the day-to-day world of site management, tenants show little dissatisfaction with their immediate landlord. Table 11 summarizes tenant perceptions of the resident managers and how satisfactorily each performs his job.

TABLE 11

SATISFACTION WITH RESIDENT MANAGER, BY PERCENTAGES

Resident Manager is:	(n=1,240) Families	(n=711) Elderly
Hard to please	11.3	10.1
Impolite	9.3	8.6
Too strict	6.3	7.6
Annoying	5.6	7.6
Stubborn	6.0	7.6
Around when needed	72.4	82.3
Resident Manager does:	(n=1,240) Families	(n=711) Elderly
Enforce rules	79.4	83.5
Know the tenant situation well	77.8	84.0
Leave the tenants alone	84.3	83.4
Act superior	17.5	10.1
Keep information from tenants	14.9	9.0
Show favoritism	13.1	7.0

Both elderly and family respondents project a similarly favorable impression of the resident manager. Rarely do more than 10 percent impute unpleasant characteristics to his behavior or personality. The only serious dispute concerns his availability in emergency circumstances: 28 percent of family tenants and 18 percent of the elderly suggest he is not always around when needed. On the basis of the foregoing results, WHA management could take pride in positive tenant assessment of its performance.

The 1973 baseline survey also sought the tenant's perception of problems of maintenance and possible residential dangers. On balance, as seen in Table 12, public housing units are perceived to be fundamentally safe from serious hazards. Elderly residents are nearly unanimous in denying the prospects of danger in their high-rise units; among tenant families, electric shock stands out as the one recurring hazard.

Routine maintenance, in general, is the one problem area within the WHA's operations. A catalog of maintenance problems and the percentages of respondents reporting no difficulties with these items appear in

Table 13. Screens, defective household equipment, inoperative plumbing and deteriorating paint on interior walls are cited as problematic by nearly half of all tenant family respondents. Almost one-third report some maintenance problems in each of the remaining areas. Once again, the elderly are overwhelmingly without complaint.

TABLE 12

PERCENTAGE OF TENANTS REPORTING NO DANGER OF ACCIDENTS INSIDE HOUSE

Hazard	(n=1,240) Families	(n=711) Elderly
Electric shock	68.9	94.0
Faulty appliances	75.3	96.3
Fire hazards	80.0	95.5
Lead poisoning	88.0	n.a.
Slippery floors/rails	81.5	93.4
No handrails	n.a.	86.2
No fire alarm system	n.a.	85.6

n.a. = not applicable

One important change traceable directly to the Wave I round of interviews was the reorganization of maintenance activities and personnel. Routine maintenance work was separated from groundskeeping activities and maintenance staff were encouraged to adopt a more responsive attitude. All told, these efforts paid off. To anticipate just one result from the Wave II round of interviews, tenants reported fewer maintenance problems in early 1974 (compared with a year earlier) and also supplied a more glowing portrait of maintenance personnel. This result is precisely what WHA had hoped to gain from systematic interview of its tenants and policies flowing directly from tenant preferences.

A Profile of Tenant Concerns

What, precisely, is the extent of unmet social service wants? Table 14 dramatically demonstrates that the overwhelming majority of tenant

TABLE 13

PERCENTAGE OF TENANTS REPORTING NO PROBLEMS WITH MAINTENANCE

Item	(n=1,240) Families	(n=711) Elderly
Replacing screens	46.0	n.a.
Painting exteriors	66.2	n.a.
Painting interiors	53.8	84.1
Repairing household equipment	46.6	83.9
Repairing plumbing	48.4	82.6
Repairing walls and floors	57.3	79.2
Replacing gates to boiler rooms	74.0	n.a.
Repairing furnace	65.8	n.a.
Repairing damage from flooding	67.2	80.6
Repairing electrical fixtures	62.0	84.6
Repairing leaky roof	69.9	84.9
Repairing elevators	n.a.	81.7
Repairing uplifts	n.a.	88.3
Repairing washers and dryers	n.a.	84.4
Installation of buzzers in maintenance offices	n.a.	82.1

n.a. = not applicable

families, elderly residents, and waiting list respondents do not consider themselves to be in *need* of substantial services or personal assistance. Only adult education and legal services are desired by more than 10 percent of the family and waiting list respondents. Otherwise, the respondents who have sought or seek the benefits supplied by social service agencies encounter no problems obtaining those services.

What about health care? Day care? Public housing resident services? Difficulties with transportation? Are the poor tenants in public housing in great need of these services? Again the answer is no. The proportion of respondents who have encountered no problem with obtaining health care appears in Table 15. The two chief difficulties for family tenants are functions of time and distance. Several of the project sites are located on the fringe areas of Wilmington wherein bus and taxi services are less readily available than in other parts of the city. Note, and this is most important, that money is not a serious problem for the overwhelming majority of tenants. The vast bulk of tenants can afford the health care services they seek; what they prefer is easier access and reduced effort in terms of time. Note, also, the similarity in response between family

TABLE 14

PERCENTAGE OF TENANTS REPORTING NO PROBLEMS WITH OBTAINING
SOCIAL SERVICES

Service	(n=1,240) Families	(n=711) Elderly	(n=121) Waiting List
Adult education	84.6	90.2	86.3
Mental health	92.5	93.8	92.2
Visiting nurses	93.9	94.6	93.0
Legal services	86.8	97.1	89.7
Family counseling	93.2	n.a.	98.2
Individual counseling	95.1	97.7	96.5
Marital counseling	97.1	99.4	98.2
Family planning	95.2	n.a.	97.4
Homemaking services	94.7	97.5	94.7
Recreational programs for the elderly	n.a.	95.3	n.a.

n.a. = not applicable

tenants and waiting list respondents: cost is simply not a problem. As we
have now come to expect, the elderly perceive few problems with
obtaining adequate health care.

TABLE 15

PERCENTAGE OF TENANTS REPORTING NO PROBLEMS WITH OBTAINING
HEALTH CARE

Problem	(n=1,240) Families	(n=711) Elderly	(n=121) Waiting List
Doctor's fees too expensive	78.8	81.1	82.9
Clinic too expensive	80.6	83.1	85.4
Drugs too expensive	77.6	78.3	82.9
Long distance and transportation	59.1	83.9	59.0
Long waiting time and lack of comfortable facilities	53.8	86.5	49.3
Staff attitude and mannerisms	72.9	97.6	94.3
Inconvenient hours	68.2	94.1	61.8
Lack of day care	89.1	n.a.	88.5

n.a. = not applicable

Recall that less than one-third of family heads of household were employed at the time of the survey. Since a very large number of the female heads have preschool-age children, it was plausible to expect that difficulties with or unavailability of satisfactory day-care facilities stood in the way of increased employment. Were these tenants out of work by choice or by force of circumstance? An answer to this question is found in Table 16: only the barest handful of tenants report any difficulty with obtaining day care for young children. Neither cost nor distance poses any problem.

TABLE 16

PERCENTAGE OF TENANTS REPORTING NO PROBLEMS WITH DAY CARE

Problem	(n=1,240) Families
Not available	92.0
Time after sign-up	92.5
Too expensive	93.7
Hours unsuitable	93.3
Facilities too crowded	93.3
No transportation	92.7
No program	95.8

Transportation is, in general, the one often-cited problem area for family tenants. Between 30 to 40 percent of these households encounter less than satisfactory transportation for such purposes as shopping, recreation, visiting friends, working, or seeing a doctor or dentist. Among the elderly, the proportion declines to about 10 percent. Again, the answer is found in the location of several project sites, which are not conveniently situated to main routes of public transportation.

One last social service program deserves mention. Attached to the WHA is a Resident Services Division, which at the time of the Wave I baseline survey consisted of about 34 full-time social service workers in the family services unit and six in the elderly services unit. One very unobtrusive measure of tenant demand for social services can be discerned in the frequency with which tenants voluntarily seek assistance from the Resident Services Division in the WHA. Of the 1,240 heads of household interviewed, only 101 reported contact with a social service worker in Resident Services; of the 711 elderly residents, only 64 affirmed contact. A mere 8 to 9 percent of WHA tenants have sought assistance from Resident Services. This, in itself, is evidence of minimal *need*.

The interview afforded the opportunity to ask these 101 and 64 persons, respectively, for their preferred manner of contact with Resident Services Division personnel. Respondents were given the choice of regular monthly intervals or a "request when needed" basis. The latter was preferred, respectively, by 86 percent of household heads and 91 percent of the elderly. Neither set wanted regular monthly visits.

Two inferences can be drawn from these responses. First, personal assistance is neither extensively sought nor obtained from the WHA's social service workers, nor do tenants report problems in obtaining services outside of WHA. Second, tenants prefer a minimum of intrusion into their private lives.

But surely public housing is not a Garden of Eden. It violates our intuitive sensibilities to believe that public housing tenants are generally content with their lot. Have these tenants no serious problems in their immediate environment? Do they seek no additional or new services of any kind?

The survey did elicit one broad area of strong tenant concern. That was crime. Table 17 shows that a majority of family tenants perceive danger from robbery or vandalism, that a near majority is concerned over drugs and possible assault, and more than one-third fear rape or having their car stolen. Moreover, the topic of crime was virtually the only area in which the elderly expressed any serious concern with life in Wilmington or its public housing. Law and order is not the monopoly of middle-class citizens; lower-class citizens have even greater cause to demand increased police protection.

Are these fears well grounded? In the two years preceding the January 1973 Wave I survey, nearly one-quarter of all family households reported themselves as victims of crime. Burglary or vandalism affected 19 percent. Nearly 45 percent of family heads believed that personal property in the housing unit was not safe if they were out of the home. We can conclude from these experiences and perceptions that the one overriding preference of the WHA's tenants is for increased security in their personal lives.

How widespread was the conviction for increased security? "Should WHA have its own security force?" In response to this question, 79 percent of family heads and 83 percent of the elderly tenants said yes.

TABLE 17

PERCENTAGE OF TENANTS REPORTING A PERCEIVED DANGER OF CRIME

Perceive a great deal or some danger of:	(n=1,240) Families	(n=711) Elderly
Being exposed to drugs	48.1	n.a.
Being robbed	64.4	40.3
Being assaulted	48.9	38.8
Being raped	37.0	29.0
Car stolen	37.6	n.a.
Vandalism	53.8	35.3

n.a. = not asked

Even 89 percent of the waiting list respondents shared this conviction. Police protection, not social services, in the eyes of our poverty-level tenants, is a basic human need, a fact of life that was unambiguously acknowledged in the Housing and Community Development Act of 1974, in Title II, Sec. 201. (a), Sec. 6 (c) (4) "(C) the establishment of effective tenant-management relationships designed to assure that satisfactory standards of *tenant security* and project maintenance are formulated and that the public housing agency (together with tenant councils where they exist) enforces those standards fully and effectively; . . ." (emphasis added).

The response of the WHA to its tenants' expressed concerns over crime and maintenance and disinterest in social service assistance, is the story of Chapter 4. There we outline the WHA's decisions, made in direct response to the survey, and we evaluate, in the tenants' own perspective, the decisions in the Wave II and Wave III reinterviews of the succeeding two years.

4

INTERVENTION AND TENANT RESPONSE

Resident response has been a relatively neglected concern in determining, influencing, or evaluating the management practices and policies that have been common in public housing in the past. Until now the literature on public housing and its management has concentrated more on administration and executive organization than on the role of management in helping residents attain the kinds of housing-related goals they desire. Apart from the physical shelter that a roof and four walls afford each tenant family, what additional housing-related goals have the WHA's tenants articulated? Extensive provision of social services? No. A high priority on personal security and protection of property? Yes. A minimally acceptable standard of unit and neighborhood maintenance? Also yes.

Public opinion polling has long influenced how candidates respond to electorates and if governments should continue, revise, or abandon current policies. Voters are evidently presumed to know their own minds and the successful politician frequently polls his constituents to assess his popularity or electoral support. It is the rare Burkean politician who turns his eyes from the benefits of polling and openly flaunts the wishes of his constituents.

The technique of public opinion polling has not been integral to the past management of public housing in America, as Lawrence Friedman so vividly made clear. The monies provided in HUD's MIP, of which the WHA was a major beneficiary, permitted for the first time a polling of public housing tenants on topics of management practices and policies. Tenants could, and did, assess which practices and policies were desired and well received, which were unwanted, misdirected, and wasteful, and which were lacking altogether. The baseline data obtained in Wave I, in which all family heads of households and all elderly residents were interviewed, was the first phase in this polling process—the assessment of current programs and the demand for new, but as yet unavailable, programs. Waves II and III of the tenant surveys, conducted with a sample of household heads and elderly residents, afforded an annual reevaluation of management decisions taken in response to resident views. This chapter tells the three stories that emerged from the application of a three-year panel of tenant opinion; the next chapter, however, will restrain our enthusiasm with a demonstration of the limits of intervention.

Story One: Resident Services

The Wave I baseline data presented in the preceding chapter must surely disabuse any reader of the notion that either family or elderly tenants have been in recent need of social services. Only the smallest handful of tenants report difficulty obtaining education, health, legal assistance, counseling, homemaking, or day-care services. Bear in mind, however, that the 1973 baseline survey presumed the widespread existence of tenant social service needs, a presumption which then justified a Resident Services Division some 34 persons strong.

This justification clearly evaporated in the face of Wave I results. Moreover, in the preceding August (1972), TransCentury completed a set of interviews with personnel in the 47 principal social service agencies operating in the Wilmington area. On the basis of these surveys and other related documents, a directory of social services was compiled and distributed to all tenants as the keystone of a systematic social service referral system. The lack of tenant demand for direct WHA provision of services, in conjunction with the compilation of the social services handbook, prompted the WHA to reduce the Resident Services Division by one-third, from 34 to 23. Direct services to tenants fell off commensurately, and the principal agencies operating in the Wilmington area assumed increased responsibility for delivery of social services to the WHA's tenants.

In view of the tenants' limited demand for resident services, why had the WHA maintained an overstaffed Resident Services Division? A first reason lay in the widespread presurvey conviction that the WHA would fall short of its mission if its black, fatherless tenant households lacked direct provision of services. A second, and perhaps more tangible, reason is that the State of Delaware was administering 75 percent/25 percent matching funds, which supported resident services. These funds are traceable to the Public Welfare Amendments of 1962, sponsored by the Kennedy administration, which initiated a category of grants to the states for social services. This law required the states to provide services to welfare recipients and authorized federal payment of 75 percent of the cost.[1] Thus the federal government paid the lion's share of the cost of the resident services program. When the state terminated the administration of these matching funds in 1973, the WHA further pared its resident services employees from 22 to 9. In the short span of a few months, management dissolved nearly three-quarters of the Resident Services Division.

The nine remaining employees were then assigned a new, more concentrated set of duties. Direct provision of services to all tenants gave way to an experiment in which a set of "excessive-cost families" were identified for special intensive attention (see Chapter 5). Apart from this experimental group of families, the general tenant now had to look outside the WHA for desired services; internal assistance was limited chiefly to referrals to outside agencies by the respective resident managers.

Did this dramatic reduction in resident services increase tenant perception of social service needs? Did it breed a hostile reaction? Table 18 explicitly justifies the decision prompted by the baseline survey. Tenant perception of service needs has declined significantly throughout the two-year period between Waves I and III, with an especially dramatic and statistically significant reduction in the final year. The average number of negative responses displayed at the bottom of the table and for succeeding tables constitutes a summary index of tenant dissatis-faction—the higher the average number of negative responses, the greater the extent of dissatisfaction on each set of questions. To attribute the reductions in dissatisfaction to the withdrawal of direct service provision is inferentially unwarranted, but we can confidently conclude that the withdrawal had no ill effects on the tenants' view of social service wants.[2]

TABLE 18

PERCENTAGE OF PANEL WHO ALWAYS OR SOMETIMES HAVE PROBLEMS WITH OBTAINING SOCIAL SERVICES

Service	*Families (n= 294)*			*Elderly (n=76)*	
	1973	1974	1975	1973	1974
Adult education	13.6	9.5	7.1	5.2	1.3
Mental health	4.8	6.1	2.7	0.0	0.0
Visiting nurses	5.8	4.8	3.7	2.6	0.0
Legal services	9.8	4.4	3.7	2.6	0.0
Family counseling	4.4	3.4	3.4	n.a.	n.a.
Individual counseling	3.4	3.4	2.7	1.3	0.0
Marital counseling	1.4	2.8	1.7	1.3	0.0
Family planning	4.1	4.1	1.7	n.a.	n.a.
Homemaking services	3.7	4.8	1.3	1.3	0.0
Recreation programs for the elderly	n.a.	n.a.	n.a.	2.6	3.9
Average number of negative responses	.53	.42	.28		

| N.S. | ** |
| ** |

n.a = not applicable
*p≤.10
**p≤.05
***p≤.01
N.S. Not Significant

A tightening budget has induced still additional reductions in the family services unit of the now miniature Resident Services Division. Apart from a Deputy Director of Resident Services, only two full-time employees work within the family services unit. Of these, one is assigned to the recently funded Target Project Program (to run from 1975 through 1977), which has as its purpose the upgrading of property and personal life in the Southbridge and Southbridge Extension projects; the other is assigned to the Comprehensive Employment and Training Act program. Any subsequent expansion of resident services is likely to depend solely on the WHA's success in procuring grants or contracts that specify additional personnel. (We should note that revenue-sharing funds from New Castle County have financed the retention of the full core of workers assigned to the elderly services unit, one of whom is assigned to each of the WHA's high-rise projects for the elderly.)

Since most tables in this chapter have identical formats, a few observations on reading them may be helpful. Each table presents the responses of family tenants for all three waves; the elderly, we recall, participated only in the first two. The tables indicate statistical significance on family tenant responses for the 1973—1974, the 1974—1975, and the 1973—1975 dyads. The smaller number of elderly respondents preclude a meaningful reporting of measures of statistical significance. Results are generally displayed in percentage form, computed on the basis of 294 family and 76 elderly tenants. Applying these remarks to Table 18 for instance, shows that the reduction in service needs between 1973 and 1974 is not statistically significant, but that the overall reduction is. The exact level of significance is specified for each dyadic relationship.

Story Two: Security

One overriding issue dominates all others in the social life of a public housing tenant in Wilmington: a desire for increased security of person and protection of property. The 1973 baseline survey indicated that nearly one-quarter of all family households had been victims of crime during the preceding two years. Reports of victimization went hand in hand with the finding that a majority of family tenants expressed fear of personal danger from robbery and vandalism, with a near majority frightened by drugs and possible assault. This evidence clearly indicates the salience of crime in the lives of the more than 1,000 tenant families who inhabit public housing in Wilmington.

Tenant perceptions of criminal risk are well-grounded in fact. The major project site of Riverside, for example, enjoyed the dubious distinction as the area with the highest crime rate in Wilmington in the summer of 1972. Residents of one project alone reported burglaries amounting to $19,000 worth of property during a six-month period in 1972. Both tenants and WHA staff generally regard police service in public housing areas as below that supplied to other areas of the city. In addition to the tenants' personal losses, the WHA estimated that property damage and vandalism to housing units approached $200,000 a year. Police coverage of public housing neighborhoods throughout 1972 was, in the eyes of its tenants, sporadic and inadequate.

To cope with this manifestly unpleasant—downright unacceptable— situation, the WHA hired in August 1972 a former Wilmington Police Department captain to design a security system. Phase One in his program consisted of a systematic examination of security systems implemented by other LHAs. This search brought the issue of firearms into the forefront of discussion. Would the WHA security force patrol armed or unarmed? The recent experience of a Wilmington police officer coming under fire in the Riverside project influenced the decision to arm the housing security force.

City administrators did not instantly applaud the prospect of an armed housing security force. The police department, in particular, did not relish the existence of a *separate* armed private security force policing the WHA properties. This issue was resolved in April 1973 when the WHA contracted with the city police department to employ off-duty policemen as housing security force officers. Once the security force had been authorized, a sum of $129,000 was earmarked in the budget for the first year's program to run from 1 April 1973 through 31 March 1974. Volunteers were sought from the city police rosters, and 20 men were selected from a list of 47 volunteers for this off-duty housing security work.

WHA thus formally contracted with the city police department for the services of 20 patrolmen at $115,000, purchased four cars and communication equipment compatible with that of the police department, and officially inaugurated active policing on 6 August 1973. A special 12-hour seminar was implemented for the off-duty officers, which focused on (1) handling family crisis situations, (2) special conditions of minorities, (3) community relations, and (4) the "cop on the beat" nature of security force work in getting to know the local residents. Improved doors, locks, and neighborhood lighting were also installed in the projects.

The police department cooperated in the WHA's efforts to monitor the effectiveness of the security force. A computerized reporting program provided a monthly summary to the Coordinator of Protective Services that listed what crimes were committed, where and when they occurred, and the financial losses involved. This information is coded by project site from city police reports.

As previously noted, the active policing commenced in August. The initial schedule of assignments placed four men on a 9:00 a.m. to 5:00 p.m. shift, and a similar set of two-man teams from 5:00 p.m. to 1:00 a.m., with a supervisor controlling each shift. An early morning 1:00 a.m. to 5:00 a.m. shift was also tried for a brief trial basis, but this had generally been a low-crime period. Specific hours in these schedules were designated for walking patrols, unless special circumstances diverted officers to more pressing duties. Although the program started slowly, in part because tenants could not identify with housing officers in Wilmington police uniforms, the initiation of a public relations program quickly contributed to their acceptance.

Indeed, the local NAACP awarded the Martin Luther King Award to one member of the force for his outstanding service. This officer was singled out for his "one-man community relations program," which included free distribution of toys, candy, and fruit to 500 children at Christmas time, and his unselfish devotion to residents of one of the projects. The significance of this award lay in the fact that a committee of blacks honored a white policeman who served an all-black project.

As the tables shortly demonstrate, the security force received broad recognition and acceptance. Its continuation depended on HUD's approval of the WHA's annual budget, however, as is true for any LHA receiving HUD operating subsidies to cover budget deficits. Negotiations with HUD in early 1974 on WHA's projected annual budget eliminated the security force budget entry of $129,000 on the presumed belief and hope that these moneys to sustain a security force might be obtained from other sources. Elimination of the security force budget was an expedient means of bringing into overall balance an otherwise unacceptable budget in deficit.

No alternative source of funds was found to maintain the full program.[3] Accordingly, the security force was reduced by two-thirds in April 1974, and these expenditures were absorbed from the WHA's general operating budget. Morning shifts were cancelled and only four officers carried out four- to eight-hour shifts between 1:00 p.m. and 1:00 a.m. This reduction increased the use of mobile patrols in place of the previously more visible walking patrols. The Coordinator of Protective Services recalls a marked increase in household burglaries and vandalism to vacant units, along with a revived drug problem, shortly after the reduction in police service.

Further cuts were made on 30 July 1974. Afternoon patrols were abolished, and service was provided only between 5:00 p.m. and 1:00

a.m. for a shortened six-day week. On 1 April 1975, the program was officially terminated for want of funds.

Police service was shifted to the city police department. The additional security protection provided within the WHA was confined exclusively to the high-rise projects for the elderly and the Southbridge and Southbridge Extension projects. HUD's modernization program allocated approximately $140,000 to install a communication system and smoke detection equipment in each of four high-rise sites for the elderly (about $110,000) and to provide rent rebates for elderly residents who served as security aides (about $29,000). A $32,000 grant funded a "youth escort" program for the elderly residents of Compton Towers, who were not included in the foregoing modernization program for the elderly. Finally, the Target Project Program included a policeman on horseback eight hours a day. Note that each of these grants was obtained with the help of the survey data that documented the tenants' desire for security.

What was the tenant response to this brief security force program? Recall that 79 percent of family heads and 83 percent of the elderly tenants replied "Yes" to the question "Should WHA have its own security force?" Wave II revealed a favorable response to the new security force. Approximately 60 percent of both family and elderly tenants were aware of its existence. Among the elderly, 55 percent of the sample of 76 persons felt the force had made public housing safer. Of the family tenants who knew of the security force's existence, over four-fifths wanted to see it continued or expanded. Virtually all respondents who came into contact with the patrol reported being well-treated.

Reductions in the security force yielded visibly different results in Wave III. The proportion of residents who knew that the WHA had a separate security force fell from 57 to 29 percent. Of this category, only 55 percent indicated that they saw members of the force more than once a week. Thus by January 1975, only about 15 percent of the family tenants reported any real security force presence in their lives. (The elderly were not interviewed in Wave III.) Tenant recognition of the security force thus comported with its chronological evolution and decay.

The diminution of this security force from its high point in January 1974, the timing of Wave II, to a mere shadow of its former strength the following January, the date of Wave III, correlates with an increase in tenant perception of criminal danger. The percentage of family tenants who felt safe at home dropped from 37 percent in 1974 to 29 percent in

1975. The corresponding reduction for feeling safe in the neighborhood was from 27 to 19 percent.

Wave III witnessed a dramatic upsurge in tenant fears of specific crimes. Table 19 shows that fear of drugs and rape had nearly tripled following the reductions in the security force, that fear of losing one's car to theft had nearly doubled, and that fear of assault, robbery, and vandalism had also markedly appreciated. Note also that elderly respondents reported an increased perception of criminal danger in each relevant category.

TABLE 19

PERCENTAGE OF PANEL REPORTING A PERCEIVED DANGER OF CRIME

Perceive a great deal or some danger of:	Families (n=294)			Elderly (n=76)	
	1973	1974	1975	1973	1974
Being exposed to drugs	44.1	28.1	75.0	n.a.	n.a.
Being robbed	57.5	59.2	78.9	32.9	53.9
Being assaulted	42.5	58.4	70.4	31.6	36.8
Being raped	40.6	22.4	62.3	18.4	19.7
Car stolen	34.4	29.9	54.8	n.a.	n.a.
Vandalism	47.9	48.3	73.8	28.9	32.9
Average number of negative responses	2.57	2.36	4.05		

| N.S. | *** |
| *** |

n.a. = not asked
*p≤.10
**p≤.05
***p≤.01
N.S. Not Significant

Without access to the full set of Wilmington police department records, we cannot correlate perceptions of increased criminal danger with an increase in the actual incidence of crime. Although intuitive impressions cannot substitute for rigorous quantitative analysis, we can report that WHA staff and tenants informally cite an increase in crime dating from the first reduction of the security force in April 1974. We might note that adult females comprise the bulk of the victims. Reduction and ultimate abolition of the security force thus most adversely affected the black females who head over 80 percent of the tenant households in the family projects.

Story Three: Residents Look at Management

The termination of direct counseling to tenants and the brief application of a housing security force represent two clear-cut instances in which resident response helped determine management policies in the WHA. A less concrete area of intervention lies in management's effort to improve the general "quality of life" in public housing, to address the areas of tenant dissatisfaction.

One important change traceable directly to the Wave I round of interviews was the reorganization of maintenance activities and personnel. Routine maintenance work was separated from groundskeeping activities and maintenance staff were encouraged to adopt a more responsive attitude. Table 20 points to the statistically significant reduction in perceived maintenance problems by 1974 among family tenants, a level sustained through the following year. Note also that the perception of maintenance problems among the sample of elderly residents fell off markedly. From the standpoint of the residents, maintenance problems appreciably declined.

Not only did perceived maintenance problems decline since the separation of maintenance and groundskeeping activities, but the newly created groundskeeping staff on its own bore few ill remarks. Table 21 shows that groundskeepers compared favorably with maintenance personnel in nearly every dimension, a distinction that widened throughout the final year of the panel. The slight deterioration in satisfaction with maintenance men may perhaps be attributable to the one-quarter reduction in maintenance staff which took place in 1974, with a corresponding fall in the quality of service. Indeed, as Table 22 indicates, the increased dissatisfaction with maintenance men in 1975 is almost wholly attributable to issues of response time, which a smaller work force would necessarily occasion, rather than personality and personal behavior. Maintenance men are simply more important in the minds of public housing tenants than social counsellors.

TABLE 20

PERCENTAGE OF TENANTS REPORTING PROBLEMS OR EMERGENCIES WITH
MAINTENANCE

	Families (n=294)			Elderly (n=76)	
Item	1973	1974	1975	1973	1974
Painting exteriors	31.9	24.5	30.3	n.a.	n.a.
Painting interiors	45.2	36.1	30.3	14.5	9.2
Repairing household equipment	50.3	36.4	35.4	15.8	5.2
Repairing plumbing	45.6	33.0	39.1	15.8	6.6
Repairing walls and floors	38.1	31.3	33.5	21.0	5.3
Replacing gates to boiler rooms	25.9	14.3	10.9	n.a.	n.a.
Repairing furnace	30.9	18.3	17.0	n.a.	n.a.
Repairing damage from flooding	31.3	22.1	18.7	18.4	3.9
Repairing electrical fixtures	35.3	19.2	18.4	13.2	2.6
Repairing leaky roofs	27.9	20.7	18.0	13.2	0.0
Repairing elevators	n.a.	n.a.	n.a.	17.1	11.8
Repairing uplifts	n.a.	n.a.	n.a.	11.8	3.9

Average number of negative responses   3.63   2.66   2.61

| *** | N.S. |

| *** |

n.a. = not applicable
*p≤.10
**p≤.05
***p≤.01
N.S. Not Significant

Accompanying the general improvement in maintenance and grounds-keeping since 1973 was an overall increase in the general livability of public housing units. When tenants were asked in the baseline survey for suggestions in proposed improvements to the housing units, new and larger washing machines emerged as the unqualified first choice. Thus the reduced dissatisfaction with appliances and size of equipment may be explained by the previous year's installation of new washing machines in some of the projects (see Table 23).

A statistically significant reduction in the perceived dangers of accidents in the house and immediate neighborhood corroborate the

TABLE 21

SATISFACTION WITH GROUNDSKEEPERS COMPARED WITH MAINTENANCE MEN
(FOR FAMILY TENANTS)

Do you agree that mainte- nance men (grounds- keepers) are:	(n=294) 1974		(n=294) 1975	
	Maintenance Men	Groundskeepers	Maintenance Men	Groundskeepers
Lazy	18.0	10.2	19.7	8.5
Messy	18.7	9.9	16.7	7.1
Cooperative (disagree)	13.6	14.3	19.0	8.5
Provide good quality work (disagree)	21.4	18.0	22.4	12.2

TABLE 22

PERCENTAGE OF FAMILIES PANEL REPORTING SATISFACTION WITH
MAINTENANCE MEN

Do you agree that maintenance men are:	(n=294) 1973	(n=294) 1974	(n=294) 1975
Lazy	25.5	18.0	19.7
Messy	18.7	18.7	16.7
Cooperative (disagree)	24.1	13.6	19.0
Provide good quality work (disagree)	28.6	21.4	22.4
Come on time (disagree)	52.4	45.2	48.3
Respond OK to emergencies (disagree)	44.9	32.0	40.8
Respond OK to routine calls (disagree)	44.9	36.4	43.5
Average number of negative responses	2.36	1.85	2.11

	***		*	

	N.S.	

*p≤.10
**p≤.05
***p≤.01
N.S. Not Significant

TABLE 23

PERCENTAGE OF PANEL REPORTING PROBLEMS OF LIVABILITY (SOMEWHAT OR SERIOUS) IN PUBLIC HOUSING

Livability Problems	Families (n=294)			Elderly (n=76)	
	1973	1974	1975	1973	1974
Appearance	30.6	27.2	22.1	7.8	2.6
Noise level	39.1	28.6	22.8	9.2	3.9
Size of equipment	39.1	21.1	15.0	2.6	0.0
Living space	34.0	28.6	27.2	6.5	5.2
Electrical outlets	36.2	23.5	21.7	0.0	1.3
Appliances	23.8	18.0	15.0	0.0	3.9
Plumbing	30.2	28.2	28.2	3.9	5.2
Average number of negative responses	2.23	1.75	1.52		

```
                                    |___***__|__*__|
                                    |_____***_____|
```

*p≤.10
**p≤.05
***p≤.01

foregoing improvements in groundskeeping and unit livability. Table 24 shows that perceived danger from faulty appliances, lead poisoning, slippery floors and stairs, blowing dirt, vacant houses, dogs, and abandoned cars all markedly diminished. These improved responses are easily correlated with more effective maintenance and grounds-keeping policies, especially the decision to board up vacant units, both to reduce vandalism and their hazardous potential to children.

A second dimension of resident response is found in the tenant's relationships with each project's resident manager, whose role assumed more importance as a link between tenants and the WHA following the withdrawal of general counseling previously offered by the Resident Services Division. Indeed, as Table 25 demonstrates, tenant opinion of resident managers fluctuated significantly in all three waves of the panel.

Note first that Wave II shows a deterioration in resident opinion of their managers, followed by a dramatic reversal in Wave III, in which the average number of negative responses per tenant is cut nearly in half.

TABLE 24

PERCENTAGE OF PANEL REPORTING PERCEIVED DANGER OF ACCIDENTS
INSIDE HOUSE AND IN NEIGHBORHOOD

Hazard	Families (n=294)			Elderly (n=76)	
	1973	1974	1975	1973	1974
Electrical shock	28.5	31.3	30.9	6.5	3.9
Faulty appliances	23.5	22.4	16.6	3.9	3.9
Fire hazards	19.4	16.3	15.7	3.9	1.3
Lead poisoning	10.1	4.1	2.1	n.a.	n.a.
Slippery floors/stairs	15.3	5.8	4.7	7.8	1.3
Play hazards	38.0	27.5	31.6	n.a.	n.a.
Blowing dirt	42.2	28.2	24.5	15.7	2.6
Vacant houses	42.9	33.7	23.8	n.a.	n.a.
Dogs	54.5	46.2	40.8	1.3	5.3
Abandoned cars	29.2	25.1	17.6	n.a.	n.a.
Dark stairways	n.a.	n.a.	n.a.	2.6	1.3

Average number of negative responses	3.04	2.41	2.09		

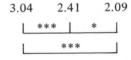

n.a. = not applicable
*$p \leqslant .10$
**$p \leqslant .05$
***$p \leqslant .01$

How can we explain this pattern of response? And what, if anything, did the WHA do when confronted with the January 1974 results?

Interviews with WHA staff pointed to the person of resident manager as the source of difficulty. First, the sexual distribution of resident managers was heavily biased in favor of men. In January 1973, 13 of 16 managers and assistant managers were male, a figure which dropped to 7 of 15 by January 1974. Nearly three-quarters of all family tenants live in the five major project sites of Eastlake, Eastlake Extension, Southbridge, Southbridge Extension, and Riverside, however, and the three resident managers at the time of the Wave II survey were still men, though each had a female assistant. It is important to recall that 84 percent of

TABLE 25

PERCENTAGE OF PANEL REPORTING PERCEPTIONS OF RESIDENT MANAGERS

Believe that resident manager is:	Families (n=294)			Elderly (n=76)	
	1973	1974	1975	1973	1974
Hard to please	7.1	12.2	5.4	6.6	1.3
Impolite	7.8	13.9	5.8	5.3	3.2
Too strict	5.8	7.1	3.4	2.6	0.0
Annoying	3.7	6.5	2.0	3.9	0.0
Stubborn	4.1	6.5	3.7	2.6	1.3
Around when needed (disagree)	25.9	23.5	17.7	7.9	5.3
Enforces the rules (disagree)	19.7	24.5	14.3	6.6	5.3
Knows the tenant situation well (disagree)	21.8	22.1	14.3	7.9	7.9
Leaves tenants alone (disagree)	13.9	17.7	13.3	14.5	6.6
Acts superior	16.7	14.6	5.8	2.6	3.9
Keeps information from tenants	15.0	12.6	6.8	2.6	14.5
Shows favoritism	15.3	16.7	5.4	2.6	6.6
Average number of negative responses	1.57	1.78	0.98		

|_ N.S. _|_ *** _|

|_____ *** _____|

*p≤.10
**p≤.05
***p≤.01

these tenant families are female-headed, and therein could be found the source of friction between tenant and resident manager.

Complaints about these resident managers, coupled with the Wave II findings presented to the WHA in summer 1974, brought about a new management policy: the assignment of female resident managers to all major family unit projects. In particular, women who had successfully served as resident managers in scattered-site housing and in several of the elderly high-rise sites were transferred to the major family projects. Additionally, another woman, one of the former assistants in a major site, was designated assistant deputy director of family units. All told then, management's response to tenant dissatisfaction ushered in the policy of installing women as resident managers in family projects. With the exception of Eastlake, as seen in Table 26, the perception of resident managers improved dramatically in each of the four remaining family unit projects.

TABLE 26

PERCEPTIONS OF RESIDENT MANAGERS BY PROJECT SITE (AVERAGE NUMBER OF NEGATIVE RESPONSES)

Project Site	N	1973	1974	1975
Eastlake	34	1.21	0.65	1.24
Southbridge	36	3.17	1.64	0.94
Eastlake Extension	25	1.40	2.08	1.24
Southbridge Extension	32	1.19	2.97	0.69
Riverside	75	2.24	1.85	0.97
Scattered site	30	0.77	2.17	1.00
Asbury Manor	11	0.55	1.64	0.82
Evans, Kennedy	7	0.57	1.29	1.43
Scattered site, Madison Garden	34	0.94	1.88	0.82
TOTAL	284	1.62	1.84	0.98

Wave III clearly demonstrates tenant approval of the new resident manager assignments. Of those who offered an opinion, 40 percent said the new manager was better than the previous one; only 6 percent said she was worse. We should point out, though, that only 41 percent of the panel answered all questions posed about resident managers in 1975. About 34 percent claimed they had never talked to or met their resident manager. At the other extreme, only 16 percent said they met with their resident manager once a month or more. Thus a majority of family tenants rarely or never talked with a resident manager. Nonetheless, the decision to employ female resident managers was successful and favorably evaluated.

Perceptions of general WHA management also registered steady improvement through 1975. By Wave III, tenants had 28 percent fewer specific complaints about WHA management than they had signified two years earlier. Marked reductions in problems associated with the position of resident manager and possible racist attitudes in the WHA led the areas of improvement.

Resident response played an important part in the three foregoing concrete instances of management intervention in the lives of Wilmington's public housing tenants. The withdrawal of direct service provision, the establishment of a housing security force (albeit short-lived), and the adoption of a new policy in filling the position of resident manager with women for all family projects—all represent successful management decisions based, in the main, on resident response obtained in the baseline and subsequent annual surveys. In each case the decision to intervene was based on resident opinion and in each case subsequent tenant evaluation of these interventions was favorable.

5

THE LIMITS TO INTERVENTION

Public housing tenants in Wilmington clearly see no need for in-house direct provision of social services, directly recognize the psychic and material benefits of increased security, and can pinpoint unwanted resident managers. In these three areas of intervention, resident response played a major role in guiding the formulation, implementation, or revisions in the policies and programs of the WHA. No longer does the WHA operating budget earmark dollars to hire social service counsellors—indeed, in July 1975 only two counsellors served family tenants and each was assigned to a special project supported outside the confines of the normal operating budget. This is truly a dramatic drop from the 34 full-time personnel who staffed the Resident Services Division three years earlier. Resident response also instigated the installation of a housing security force, which met widespread approval until curtailed by budget limitations. Finally, a policy of appointing female resident managers in the family projects was again based on tenant response.

Resident response also played a part in prompting management *not* to undertake programs envisaged in the original proposal submission to HUD of 26 October 1971. In addition to an automated management information system and extensive information system of tenant preferences, the original "Wilmington System" also featured a tenant organization component. But the data in the baseline survey convincingly established that Wilmington's public housing residents did not want to be organized in 1973 (as they perhaps did a few years earlier in Wilmington and elsewhere). Tenant organization, as an initial component in the package of proposals that comprised the MIP in Wilmington, was formally abandoned.[1] The decision to cast off this concrete goal rested, as the foregoing positive interventions had rested, on tenant preferences.

We have told a story to this point of well-conceived programs that were based on the views of residents and received widespread approval upon implementation. We have also indicated that programs can be abandoned as well as inaugurated, that tenants know both what they *do* want and what they *do not* want. The expectation that tenants would welcome tenant organization efforts proved unfounded, having perhaps rested on a faulty view that linked citizen participation, democratic political theory, and executive decision-making. Although tenants welcomed technical assistance in crime control and maintenance/grounds-keeping, they did not welcome assistance in social service areas and tenant organization. Systematic gathering and analysis of resident opinion, in the manner that market research aids any commercial enterprise in the design, marketing, or withdrawal of its products from the marketplace, enabled the WHA to implement new programs in the presence of tenant demand and abandon others for which little or no demand was present. The model of commercial market research seems, in retrospect, more useful to an LHA in making decisions on behalf of tenants than the overinvolved, unbusinesslike character of the citizen participation model.

Excessive-Cost Program

The original proposal submission listed three basic objectives of the MIP: improved management, improved resident services, and increased cost-effectiveness. To this point we have talked a lot about resident services and management decisions that took full advantage of an annual survey of resident opinion. We have not yet, however, addressed the results of efforts to increase the cost-effective provision of housing services, a topic of significant importance given the "fiscal crisis in public housing."

Problem tenants are thought by many to be a contributing factor in public housing's losing struggle to keep costs within revenues, indeed, to keep large operating deficits from growing larger. Issues of tenant selection and problem families grew in prominence throughout the 1960s as the working poor moved out of public housing and the dependent poor moved in. It is commonly believed that problem families pose higher costs for LHAs than nonproblem families. Although scholars are not unanimous in what attributes comprise *problem families*, a large and growing body of writings points to the pathological character of the multiproblem family as one that displays "disorganized social functioning" and that may inflict problems upon immediate neighbors.[2] The completion of the 1973 baseline registration survey of all family tenants afforded the WHA an opportunity both to test the allegation that multiproblem families are indeed a chief source of excessive costs and to set up an experimental situation in which these "excessive-cost" families might receive special assistance and counseling in a concerned effort to reduce costs.

Two analytical steps preceded this cost-control experiment. First it was necessary to identify the families that clearly imposed above-average costs on the WHA and, second, to determine if "excessive-cost" families are indeed multiproblem families. The 23-page survey instrument used in Wilmington had specifically included an entire battery of questions on such topics as self-esteem, social functioning, and the other factors that typically are thought to comprise valid measures of multiproblem families.

One innovation in the MIP facilitated this investigation—the installation of a monthly computer tenant-billing system for both rent and maintenance charges. In the ideal world of cost-effective public housing, all tenant charges would be paid on time and operating revenues would exactly match operating costs. The Brooke amendments and inflation put an end to the latter norm, and tenant behavior stymies the former. In the 1973 fiscal year, for example, the WHA estimates that $94,500 in excessive maintenance costs alone were not recovered from tenants. Table 27 quantifies the average rental and maintenance delinquency charges for the 1,000 family household heads who lived continuously in WHA units between August 1973 and February 1975. (Of the original sample of 1,240 household heads interviewed in Jauary 1973, exactly 240 had moved out in the interim two-year period, and thus their delinquent charges are omitted in this analysis.) Note that total arrears in August 1973 approached $75,000 for these 1,000 households, a figure that increased by $20,000, or $20 per household, by February 1975. Thus the average tenant household imposed an arrears cost of approximately $75 on the WHA in August 1973.

TABLE 27

AVERAGE DELINQUENT CHARGES

	August 1973	March 1974	February 1975	Change 73–75	Statistical Significance of Change
(n=1,000)					
Rent in arrears	$66.00	74.66	84.24	+18.24	p≤.001
Maintenance charges	8.49	10.37	10.56	+2.07	N.S.
Total arrears	74.49	85.03	94.80	+20.31	p≤.001

Averages by themselves cannot capture the variation in individual performance, an essential determination in isolating any given set of above-average individuals. What proportion of tenants have no arrears whatsoever? What proportion are well above average? Table 28 provides a first cut at these questions. Thirty-five percent of all households were fully paid up in rental and maintenance charges in August 1973, a figure that steadily increased throughout the life of the MIP. The proportion that owed over $100 remained constant at about one-fourth of the tenant population.

There was of course some shifting within categories, as seen in Table 29. Of those who owed no arrears in August 1973, 58 percent were

TABLE 28

DISTRIBUTION OF TOTAL DELINQUENT CHARGES

		August 1973	March 1974	February 1975
		(n=1,000)		
	$ 0.00	35%	37%	41%
Total arrears	$1 — $100	41	40	34
	Over $100	24	24	25
	TOTAL	100%	101%	100%

still fully paid up in February 1975, but 11 percent had incurred arrears in excess of $100. Of those who maintained large arrears in 1973, fully one-quarter were out of debt to the WHA 18 months later. As the middle row in the table depicts, one-quarter of the tenants with middle-range arrears had shifted into the high arrears category, compared with 35 percent who eliminated all arrears. Thus the history of the MIP shows both improvements and deterioration in the fiscal integrity of household tenants.

TABLE 29

ARREARS BALANCE OVER TIME

		Total Arrears (August 1973)		
		$0.00. (n=347)	$1–$100 (n=413)	Over $100 (n=240)
Total arrears (February 1975)	$0.00	58%	35%	25%
	$1 – $100	31	40	28
	Over $100	11	25	47
		100%	100%	100%
		Gamma = .44		

Obviously, improvements in arrears balances is more to the liking of management than deterioration; however, the major point of the foregoing is to highlight the wide-ranging differences among households in family projects, a first requirement in establishing the existence of "excessive-cost" families. For the purpose of an experiment in which a concerted effort could be undertaken to reduce large delinquent rental and maintenance charges, an excessive-cost family was defined as one identified by an Excessive-Cost Index formula.[3] The Excessive-Cost Index consisted of four key components: (1) rent in arrears, (2) honoring payback agreement, (3) property abuse, and (4) maintenance fee in arrears. The first two components combined to yield a rent-delinquency factor; the third and fourth similarly combined to give an excessive-maintenance factor. Rent delinquency was computed by multiplying the average monthly rent billed delinquent tenants—$47.00—by the tenant's likelihood of paying off the rent in arrears debt—estimated at 50 percent. The excessive-maintenance factor combined both actual maintenance fee in arrears along with the value of placing a living unit back into good condition after a tenant vacated. Application of the formula yielded 163 families that imposed high, intolerable excessive costs on the WHA. Any social experimentation on holding down excessive costs ought to involve these 163 target families. By September 1973, then, the first requirement had been met: 163 families had been identified as contributing excessive costs to the WHA.

Were these 163 families the multiproblem families that had tradition-ally been considered the financial thorn in the side of the LHAs' efforts to balance their budgets? Generally, multiproblem families have been defined as being victims of a combination of problems involving chronic need, resistance to treatment, suspicion of authority, and alienation from the community. These families seem to share an inability to deal with the variety of problems that affect their lives, both personally and environ-mentally. What indeed was the precise relationship between families with extensive social problems and families who cause excessive cost to an LHA? Unless multiproblem families were excessive-cost families, intensive provision of social services to multiproblem families need not necessarily reduce costs to the LHA.

Though we do not reproduce our analysis here, we could find *no* systematic link between multiproblem and excessive-cost families. Some multiproblem families posed no excessive costs and some excessive-cost families were not multiproblem. This analysis disconfirmed any notion that multiproblem families cause excessive costs to the WHA. It became clear, therefore, that the focus of special efforts to reduce costs must be changed to providing intensive assistance to excessive-cost families, rather than to multiproblem families.[4]

The original excessive-costs experiment designated 60 experimental and 60 control group families drawn from the universe of 163 identified by application of the Excessive-Cost Index formula. Of the original group of 60 experimental families, randomly drawn from the universe of 163 high-cost families, four had vacated their units, leaving an actual list of 56 participant families with which to begin the experiment in mid-November 1973.

Each of the social workers in the family services unit of the Resident Services Division was assigned from eight to ten families. After each worker was familiar with biographical data on his or her assigned families in the experimental group, contacts were initiated. By early December, most families had been seen by the workers, who began to compile case reports on such topics as housekeeping habits of the families, what transpires during the contacts, what realistically might help these families reduce costs to the WHA, and other general observations. These social workers were to provide help *exclusively* to the experimental families through such means as referrals, counseling, or other liaison services. The experimental families were not told that they had been selected for specialized attention by Resident Services because they had been identified as tenants causing excessive costs to the WHA.

Early case reports corroborated the statistical finding that high-cost families are not necessarily multiproblem families. For example, neat and tidy housekeepers are often no less costly to an LHA than sloppy and untidy ones.

The excessive-cost family experiment was very well conceived in design. It was not, however, equally well implemented. High turnover of staff workers, coupled with weak supervision of their efforts, distorted the true experimental design of the program. Within but a few months of the program's inception, the five staff workers had been reduced to three and each worker's case load became excessive. The program also suffered from the lack of steady, continuous supervision: by September 1974, the experiment was under its third supervisor. In particular, between June and August 1974, the project supervisor had in effect subverted the carefully controlled experiment when she referred all resident calls to staff workers, who then had no time to carry out their responsibilities with the target group of experimental families. Her rationale for delivering services to any resident placing a request was the moral conviction that withholding services is wrong. As a result of the difficulties encountered in implementation, most of the experimental group families saw at least three and sometimes more than three different members of the family services unit.

Table 30 summarizes the results of the excessive-cost experiment; it lists the average rental and maintenance balance in arrears for the control and experimental families at the beginning of the experiment in November 1973 and the end, 15 months later, in February 1975. Note first that the original group of 60 experimental and control families had dwindled to 36 to 39 families respectively. Note also from the table that these high-cost families have delinquent balances far greater than the tenant population as a whole (see Table 27).

TABLE 30

AVERAGE DELINQUENT BALANCES FOR EXPERIMENTAL AND
CONTROL-GROUP FAMILIES

	November 1973	February 1975
Rent in arrears		
Experimental (n=36)	$179.61	$201.25
Control (n=39)	201.77	225.36
Maintenance in arrears		
Experimental (n=36)	23.19	19.69
Control (n=39)	25.77	26.76
Total balance in arrears		
Experimental (n=36)	202.81	220.94
Control (n=39)	227.54	252.13

To infer that the program had a significant impact required the observation that the change in the experimental group was greater than the change in the control group and in the desired direction, a difference that must be statistically significant. Although Table 31 shows that the increase in the total arrears balance of the experimental group is less than that of the control group, all differences in the table are statistically insignificant. Indeed, the combination of recession and inflation experi-

TABLE 31

COMPARISON OF EXPERIMENTAL AND CONTROL-GROUP CHANGE IN
DELINQUENT BALANCE (NOVEMBER 1973 TO FEBRUARY 1975)

	Experimental (n=36)	Control (n=39)	Statistical Significance of Change
Change in:			
Rent arrears	+$21.64	+$23.59	N.S.
Maintenance balance in arrears	−3.50	+1.00	N.S.
Total arrears	$18.14	$24.59	N.S.

enced through this 15-month period makes difficult any evaluation of this program's effect on reducing tenant costs to the WHA.

The control and experimental groups were also compared on a number of perceptual and behavioral dimensions that might contribute to or reflect the tenant's ability to reduce costs to the WHA. Again, the pattern is one of no program impact. We cannot infer that the specialized attention afforded experimental families in the Excessive-Cost Program—albeit imperfectly—affected money management, employment, satisfaction of service needs, or attitudes toward the WHA. The only interesting difference between the two groups is that the program participants had *more* complaints about public housing, for reasons we do not understand.

Wave III of the panel revealed the extent to which the rigorous experimental design of the Excessive-Cost Program was not faithfully carried out. When asked whether a social service worker ever comes to visit them, 53 percent of the experimental group replied "no." Moreover, 7 percent of the control group said "yes." Thus just over half of the experimental families claimed that they did not receive the specialized attention integral to the program.

The point is that this specific exercise or any social experiment that required rigorous and faithful adherence to all procedures of implementation is not a likely candidate for success.[5] The decision to mount an Excessive-Cost Program, although based on valid survey data, was perhaps stretching the limits to successful intervention outside the feasible.

Maintenance-Incentive Program

A second experiment, a maintenance-incentive program, was also developed to cope with the entire family tenant population, to reduce the maintenance costs for which the WHA charges but often fails to collect, beyond normal wear and tear.

Recall in Table 27 that the average aggregate delinquent maintenance charges for family tenants exceeds $10,000 in any given month. On top of this number should be placed the charges that "skip-outs" never pay. The cumulative cost of deferred maintenance must sooner or later be reckoned with, as is evidenced in HUD's new modernization program of large grants for Target Project Programs in selected LHAs to catch up on deferred maintenance. (WHA received $1.3 million to modernize South-bridge and Southbridge Extension under the 1974 Target Project Program and Modernization Program.)

Reduced maintenance costs can thus heartily contribute to the fiscal solvency of an LHA. The WHA, in this vein, proposed the introduction of a maintenance-incentive scheme that would accord rent credits to tenants who incurred reduced maintenance costs. In April 1973, the submission date of WHA's second-year work plan for the MIP, the WHA calculated the average maintenance cost per family unit at $22 per month, or $264 per year. This runs to an annual total of more than $625,000, or approximately 25 percent of its total operating budget. The plan called for the development of a formula that would return a proportion of maintenance-cost savings to tenants who incurred lower than average maintenance costs, partly by maintaining their own units on a day-to-day basis.

An illustration might be helpful. Suppose a tenant inflicts only $64 in maintenance charges throughout the course of a year. The incentive formula would then calculate some sharing between the LHA and tenant of the $200 savings, a portion of which might be applied toward the tenant's rent.

This proposed cost-saving program never got off the ground.[6] The reason is that some tenants have no incentive to request any maintenance work at all *if* they prefer to purchase other goods and services with the money they now spend on fixing up their units beyond normal wear and tear, and *if* they do not mind deterioration of their units. Put another way, the value of the potential rent reduction is not worth the effort that some tenants must expend in do-it-yourself maintenance. Since the greatest savings are to be obtained from the tenants with high maintenance costs who are least interested in the rental credit incentive, there was little point in pursuing the effort. Thus the incentives to which some tenants were likely to respond led management to abort what seemed, in principle, a good idea to bring operating costs more in line with revenues.

It is hard to say which interventions are likely to succeed, which may fail either in design or implementation, and which become quickly unrealistic between thought and inception upon further examination of the incentives tenants face. One thing is certain, though. In the absence of systematic information on tenant preferences, management will find it difficult to provide services tenants want—which in Wilmington meant security, not social services. These may or may not be universal goals of public housing tenants elsewhere, but that question requires the information that only systematic interviewing can supply.

6

PUBLIC HOUSING AND PUBLIC POLICY

In 1949 the Congress mandated a "decent home" for every American family. The low and moderate income, in particular, had been given a first boost with the inception of low-rent public housing 12 years earlier. But nearly 40 years of legislation, appropriations, construction, and promising talk finds less than one-tenth of the Americans financially eligible for public housing. And especially the low-income, fatherless, large-family, black, female-headed household stood to benefit, however unevenly, from what might have otherwise been a steady expansion of new public housing construction. The overwhelming majority of low-income families in "need" of decent housing can no longer look toward public housing as its means of "decent housing," but must either rely upon its own devices in the perhaps less attractive and higher-priced private market or await some new program of demand subsidies such as the rental-assistance payments scheme set forth in Section 8 of the 1974 Housing and Community Development Act. Unless one of these new alternatives directly serves many low-income large families, the declining status and condition of public housing most harms some of the very worst-off and ill-housed sections of the American population.

Research, analysis, recommendation, and politics all intertwine in the business of making public policy. It is important, therefore, to first state what this book *is not*, and then go on to what this book *is*. It is not a search for some utopian program of public housing that will magically insure the construction and maintenance of thousands, or perhaps millions, of additional units to house the entire lower-income segment of the American population. This is patently unrealistic and prohibitively expensive. It is not an *apologia* for the nation's LHAs and any inefficient practices they pursue in the management of a public housing operation. In particular, it is not a justification for the present incentive system that the operating-costs subsidy represents, which removes any interest a housing authority may have in getting its books out of the red. Nor is it likewise supportive of the Brooke amendments, which make it impossible for a public housing agency to charge and collect an economic rent. It is not a defense of the "culture of poverty," of the pathological tendency to violent and destructive behavior that Rainwater's lower-class blacks inflict on "federal slums." If it is necessary to police these citizens rigorously to protect the public investment in low-rent housing, it should be done. Tenants have responsibilities, too. They must pay their rent on time or be evicted. Nor must tenants be allowed to inflict a steady barrage of vandalism on the projects.[1]

What, then, is this book? It is, first, a pitch that we reject all talk about pathology and the "culture of poverty," and talk, instead, about individual preferences. That the preferences of poor people are for them as reasonable as the preferences of middle-income people are for middle-income people. And most important, that these rational preferences of poor public housing residents can sensibly and effectively inform public housing management—there is no "need" for social services in the attack on any culture of poverty, but there is a need for the personal security all Americans seek. And there is also a need, in the economic sense of rationality, to impose costs and penalties on those who engage in willfully destructive behavior instead of seeking to attack the so-called underlying social conditions that many social analysts cite to rationalize this unsocial conduct. Finally, this book is cognizant of the political realities within which all talk of housing for the poor takes place and the constraints such realities impose on public housing and its real or potential alternatives. Perhaps the main message of this three-year study of public housing tenants in Wilmington is the limited conviction that the existing stock of public housing and its current management is, of itself, a public policy issue that merits serious debate, and that the rhetoric of equity and fairness threatens to drown out serious discussion of how best to use this existing stock.

Although the intellectual crisis in public housing is chiefly a verbal assault on its proponents, administrators, and tenants, it has helped induce a very real financial crisis. At its worst extreme, it threatens to destroy the massive investment we now have in public housing. Inadequate appropriations, impounded funds, the rental ceilings imposed by the Brooke amendments, bureaucratic obstacles imposed by HUD precluding prompt release of operating-costs subsidies and other public housing-related funds, coupled with a tarnished image, has forced many of the nation's public housing agencies to defer maintenance and use up fiscal reserves. In the process, the existing housing stock is threatened with irreversible deterioration, e.g., witness the dynamiting of Pruitt-Igoe, and virtually no new construction is undertaken. As the search goes on for new alternatives to housing the poor, an already viable program is financially choked to death. Public policy views public housing as a social disaster and a public eyesore, even as tenants speak in favor of it and potential tenants clamor to get in.

The prospects for public housing in today's political economy are, to understate the case, bleak. The Housing and Community Development Act of 1974 extends HUD's annual contributions contract authority by an annual figure of $150 million for new construction, which in the first fiscal year following the Act was disbursed chiefly on pre-Act commitments. An effort to expand this annual contributions contract authority to build, rehabilitate, or lease additional public housing units by $300 million was vetoed by President Ford in June 1975. Subsequent appropriations for new public housing contracts have been in the small magnitudes of $50 to $85 million. The prospects for any dramatic expansion in the stock of public housing, either in the form of new construction, rehabilitation of existing stock, or the leasing of private dwellings, are dim. It is instructive to read the President's fiscal year 1976 budget on this point.

> Section 8 of the Housing and Community Development Act of 1974, . . .
> replaced the leased housing program with the lower income housing
> assistance program. This new program will increase significantly the role
> of private owners who participate in that they will own, operate, and
> maintain units leased to lower income families. Tenants who live in
> privately owned leased existing housing will have the opportunity to select
> the unit in which they choose to live and will make rental payments
> directly to the private landlord. . . .
> It is anticipated that the new Section 8 program will be used as the

primary vehicle for providing housing assistance to lower income families in 1975 and 1976. Authority will be available to process up to 400,000 units in both 1975 and 1976. However, because the program will not be available for the full year during 1975, it is estimated that no more than 200,000 units will actually be processed.[2]

Less than 100,000 lower-income families had been certified for Section 8 housing assistance by January 1977—difficulties in starting up any new program usually preclude meeting target dates, and Section 8 is no different in this regard. Indeed, the United States government has met its low-income housing production targets, and with some irony at that, in the early Nixon years and rarely at any other time. Although the promise of several hundred thousand units of Section 8 housing is legislated, it *effectively* replaces the reality of an expanding public housing stock. The budget's projection of 200,000 units of assisted lower-income housing in 1975 and 400,000 in 1976 compares with an estimate of 38,000 additional units of LHA-owned housing in 1975 and a mere 6,000 in 1976.

The object of this book is not to debate the respective merits or faults of the Section 8 housing-assistance payments scheme, rent certificates, direct housing-allowance payments, or a general cash grant to poor people, in comparison with the good and bad features of low-rent public housing. America's past, present, and future housing policy is a mixture of old and new production and demand subsidies each of which only *partially* houses its target population. Until one or more of these housing subsidy programs for lower-income families *effectively* replaces public housing, or until the government decides to get out of the housing subsidy business altogether, the promises contained in new legislation and the unrealistic debates that go on in university corridors do not successfully maintain and manage an ever-aging stock of public housing.

Public Housing in Wilmington: A Recapitulation

Public housing has been a viable program in Wilmington. To say that this program is efficient is to say that scarce funds are expended only for the services that the tenants show they want, that no funds are wasted on alleged needs which don't exist. Public housing, in Wilmington at least, satisfies the housing needs of low-income persons, except when the program is diverted from its main task of providing housing to the tangential task of supplying a battery of services that assaults the "culture of poverty."

Public housing is in crisis because no one has heretofore asked tenants and potential tenants if they regard public housing as a successful solution to their housing needs. Asking this in Wilmington has yielded unambiguous evidence of the success of public housing, its attractiveness to current and potential tenants, and the supreme importance of the preferences of tenants in the management and policy-making of LHAs. The latter message, moreover, extends the LHA's ability to secure additional grants on the basis of accurate information—that tenants desire increased security in their lives, not an overdose of traditional social services.

The Wilmington experience stands in stark contrast to Roger Starr's analysis of the dependent poor as a chief cause in the failure of public housing. His argument simply does not hold up in the face of the WHA's experience, in which effective housing has been provided to presumed problem families. The "culture of poverty" causes no more failure in public housing than in private housing. The fact that poor black families with many teenage children live in a social milieu marked by vandalism and punctuated by violence is not a necessary correlate of "crisis" in public housing—no more so than in private housing. Moreover, this particular feature of life in public housing requires both recognition and resolution. The Target Projects Program announced in mid-1974, which combines modernization funds with provision for *increased security*, is one step in the right direction.

How widespread is tenant satisfaction with public housing outside Wilmington? How effective might other LHAs be, properly armed with knowledge of their tenants' preferences? The answers to these and other questions require a full reassessment of current thinking about public housing and a systematic analysis of the Urban Institute's surveys of managers, directors, and tenants in 120 LHAs nationwide. These data have been used as the basis for HUD's new performance-funding system for paying the operating-costs subsidies and have yielded, thus far, one major publication.[3] These data include responses of 6,000 residents at 400 housing projects on a broad range of questions, complete analysis of which would demonstrate the extent to which Starr's thesis or the one presented in this book is the more valid and applicable. To this point, however, the Urban Institute has only presented data aggregated to the

LHA level and only made comparisons between LHAs. It seems important, then, that we have household-level findings, from which we can discern a truly representative tenant assessment of public housing. But the thesis of Wilmington suggests caution in abandoning the public housing approach to low-income persons in the absence of this systematic comparative exposition, one that might reveal widespread national tenant satisfaction despite the intellectual crisis.

Rethinking the Issue

The tarnished image of public housing owes much to the glamor and publicity accorded the few horror stories that have emerged from St. Louis, New York, Chicago, and other big cities. It is our contention, though, that these few horror stories misrepresent the general picture of low-rent public housing in the United States in the mid-1970s. Indeed, what most people believe to be the case in public housing, influenced by photos of Pruitt-Igoe crumbling to earth, is demonstrably not true. Over three million people live in public housing. For every hundred units that are being torn down, tens of thousands remain intact and continue to house low-income Americans. Although a few housing authorities have been victimized by well-publicized rent strikes and the vision of disgruntled tenants, the fact is that every study we can find which reports tenants' views indicates that about 80 percent prefer public housing to their former private slum housing; moreover, those who lead rent strikes do so not in pursuit of well-defined alternatives to public housing but perhaps to attain reductions in rent or an increase in housing-related services. It is probably correct to hypothesize, though we lack direct evidence, that the percentage of residents in public housing who are satisfied with their dwelling units is as high as the percentage of all residents in private housing who are happy with their homes or apartments, and in all likelihood this percentage is higher when compared with attitudes of privately housed lower income groups.

Since 1937 we have had a program that supplies housing for poor people. Although limited in scope to a small fraction of the eligible population, it has, by and large, succeeded in its housing goals. But this program was subverted in the 1960s by a myriad of great-society endeavors that set out to alleviate, if possible eliminate, the culture of poverty—not poverty itself, but the *imputed* social service needs of the poor.

If the nation is to invest public resources in subsidized housing for poor people, it should acknowledge that poor people act like poor people. It should build housing for them that takes into account the required maintenance and police programs to deal with that fact. It should forget about the "culture of poverty."

What is the policy agenda for public housing? First, the program must be seen only as a housing subsidy. Local housing agencies are neither designed nor equipped—nor should they be—to provide a broad range of social services of which housing is but one part. Second, income limits for admission and eviction should be raised along with the lifting of rent-to-income ceilings imposed by the Brooke amendments: these two changes would allow public housing agencies to charge a more nearly economic rent and reduce their dependence on the operating-costs subsidy. Income maintenance of poor families should not be the responsibility of LHAs; this task rightly belongs to federal, state, or local income-assistance agencies. Efficient management should be rewarded by allowing LHAs to accumulate budget surpluses; profligate management ought not to be rewarded with large subsidies for operating, capital, and modernization costs.

Third, costly penalties should be imposed on irresponsible and destructive tenants—if for no other reason than to prevent injury to life and property of other rent-paying, law-abiding tenants. A policy that discourages vandalism and rental delinquency by imposing costs on tenants is more likely to succeed than one that seeks to ameliorate the social conditions which allegedly cause this irresponsible and destructive behavior.

Finally, analysts, critics, and planners must recognize that no panacea sits over the horizon that is going to house the several million persons now in public housing, not unless the federal government reverses 40 years of practice and suddenly makes available the requisite billions. The plain truth is that public spending for housing low-income persons has and will accommodate only a small fraction of the eligible target population, and that the present public housing program will continue to house more than three million persons for some time to come, regardless of any major new housing policy initiatives. We must not, therefore, invert the logic of equity and fairness to punish present tenants of public housing. This rhetoric must not obscure the issue of how best to manage the present program, even as we acknowledge the misuse of past resources. Careful consideration of equitable housing subsidies does not repair broken window panes.

NOTES

Preface

1. Lawrence M. Friedman, *Government and Slum Housing: A Century of Frustration* (Chicago: Rand McNally, 1968), pp. 144−145. (italics added)

2. See Robert Sadacca, Suzanne B. Loux, Morton L. Isler, and Margaret J. Drury, *Management Performance in Public Housing* (Washington, D.C.: The Urban Institute, 1974), p. 1. This volume reports a preliminary analysis of data collected from almost 9,000 interviews with staff and tenants in 120 carefully chosen Local Housing Authorities stratified by size. Comparisons are made only between authorities on the topic of management performance.

Introduction

1. Albert A. Walsh, "Is Public Housing Headed for a Fiscal Crisis?" *Journal of Housing* 26, No. 2, February 1969, pp. 64−71.

2. Roger Starr, "Which of the Poor Shall Live in Public Housing?" *The Public Interest*, Number 23, Spring 1971, pp. 116−124.

3. Frank de Leeuw, *Operating Costs in Public Housing: A Financial Crisis* (Washington, D.C.: The Urban Institute, 1969).

4. Nathaniel S. Keith, *Politics and the Housing Crisis Since 1930* (New York: Universe Books, 1973).

5. Leonard Freedman, *Public Housing: The Politics of Poverty* (New York: Holt, Rinehart and Winston, 1969).

6. Lee Rainwater, *Behind Ghetto Walls* (Chicago: Aldine, 1970).

Chapter 1

1. *1974 HUD Statistical Yearbook* (Washington, D.C.: U.S. Government Printing Office), pp. 61, 102. In 1971, for example, only 42 percent of the cost borne by government appears explicitly in HUD appropriations and expenditures records. Another 36 percent of the cost to government is attributable to the tax exempt status of the interest earned on local authority bonds, and another 22 percent is attributable to the difference between full local property taxes and the smaller payments made by local housing authorities to local governments in lieu of taxes. See *Housing in the Seventies. A report of the National Housing Policy Review.* U.S. Department of Housing and Urban Development (Washington, D.C.: U.S. Government Printing Office, 1974), p. 123.

2. *Housing in the Seventies, p. 125.*

3. *1974 HUD Statistical Yearbook*, pp. 98–99.

4. *1971 HUD Statistical Yearbook* (Washington, D.C.: U.S Government Printing Office), p. 146.

5. Henry J. Aaron, *Shelter and Subsidies. Who Benefits from Federal Housing Policies?* (Washington, D.C.: Brookings Institution, 1972), pp. 111–112.

6. *1974 HUD Statistical Yearbook*, p. 107.

7. *Housing in the Seventies*, p. 152.

8. Henry J. Aaron, *Shelter and Subsidies*, p. 120. For a classic study of the political elements in planning public housing, see Martin Meyerson and Edward C. Banfield, *Politics, Planning, and the Public Interest. The Case of Public Housing in Chicago* (New York: Free Press, 1955). For an analysis of the housing problems of welfare recipients in New York, including those in public housing, see George S. Sternlieb, *The Ecology of Welfare: Housing and the Welfare Crisis in New York City* (New Brunswick: Transaction Books, 1973).

9. *Housing in the Seventies*, p. 28.

10. Richard F. Muth, *Public Housing: An Economic Evaluation* (Washington, D.C.: American Enterprise Institute for Public Policy Research, 1973), p. 13.

11. *Housing for the Elderly. A Status Report.* Special Committee on Aging, United States Senate, 93d Congress, 1st Session (Washington, D.C.: U.S. Government Printing Office, 1973), p. 8. This report states that waiting lists for the elderly for public housing number 32,000 in New York City and over 12,000 in Chicago.

12. *Housing in the Seventies*, pp. 127–128. For a somewhat different analysis of these numbers, see *Critique of "Housing in the Seventies."* Housing and Urban Affairs Subcommittee of the Senate Committee on Banking, Housing, and Urban Affairs, 93d Congress, 2d Session (Washington, D.C.: U.S. Government Printing Office, 1974),

pp. 35–36. This does not mean that the recipient valued the subsidy at $1,000 worth of housing benefits, but only that $1,000 of taxpayers' money was spent supplying recipients in this income range with housing services.

13. *Housing in the Seventies,* p. 154. See also 1974 *HUD Statistical Yearbook,* p. 61.

14. For evidence of this effect in public housing in Wilmington see "Part II: Analysis of Predictor Variables for the Applicant Predictor Model" (26 February 1974), p. 61 in *Resident Referral Transfer Document Draft, Vol. II* (Wilmington Housing Authority, May 1975). This analysis shows that only 3 percent of "high excess cost" tenants were 56 years of age or older, compared with 73 percent who were 35 or younger.

15. A legal history of public housing legislation can be found in Lawrence M. Friedman, *Government and Slum Housing: A Century of Frustration* (Chicago: Rand McNally, 1968); Leonard Freedman, *Public Housing: The Politics of Poverty* (New York: Holt, Rinehart and Winston, 1969); and Robert M. Fisher, *Twenty Years of Public Housing* (New York: Harper, 1959). Our discussion in this section relies heavily on the accounts these authors present.

16. See Lawrence M. Friedman, "Public Housing and the Poor," in Jon Pynoos, Robert Schafer, and Chester W. Hartman (eds.), *Housing Urban America* (Chicago: Aldine, 1973), pp. 451 –452.

17. For a review of this migration pattern see Charles Tilly, Wagner D. Jackson, and Barry Kay, *Race and Residence in Wilmington, Delaware* (Teachers College, Columbia University, 1965).

Chapter 2

1. See Lee Rainwater, *Behind Ghetto Walls* (Chicago: Aldine, 1970), and "The Lessons of Pruitt-Igoe," *The Public Interest* No. 8, Summer 1967, pp. 116–126; see also Roger Starr, "Which of the Poor Shall Live in Public Housing?" *The Public Interest* No. 23, Spring 1971, pp. 116–124.

2. A high vacancy rate in public housing need not necessarily signal its unattractiveness to potential tenants; it may simply signal poor management performance in releasing a vacancy. And the high vacancy rate in the Pruitt and Igoe projects applied to the smaller units; the larger units stayed continuously in high demand. A number of smaller units were converted into larger, multibedroom units. For a full description of all the St. Louis Housing Authority's nine conventional projects and the history of their occupancy patterns, see Eugene J. Meehan, *Public Housing Policy, Convention Versus Reality* (New Brunswick: Center for Urban Policy Research, 1975), pp. 32 –41, 49 –51, 54 –56, 63. Meehan points out that the high vacancy rate in 1967 and succeeding years applied to some but not all of the projects and that the initial significant decrease in occupancy in 1959 in five of the projects, from which three recovered, was due to a very serious increase in criminal activity in the projects. The high vacancy rates in the Pruitt and Igoe projects, each exceeding 1,000 units in size, present a misleading picture of occupancy

patterns in the remaining seven projects, many of which were invariably well over 90 percent full.

3. See James Heilbrun, *Urban Economics and Public Policy* (New York: St. Martin's Press, 1974), p. 271.

4. Rainwater, "The Lessons of Pruitt-Igoe," pp. 119–120.

5. Rainwater, *Behind Ghetto Walls*, p. 11.

6. Meehan, *Public Housing Policy*.

7. Ibid., pp. 35–36, 64–65, 76.

8. Ibid., p. 77.

9. Ibid., p. 78.

10. Ibid., p. 128.

11. Ibid., p. 67.

12. Ibid., p. 74.

13. Ibid., p. 134.

14. Ibid., p. 37.

15. D. W. Drakakis-Smith explicitly rejects the "culture of poverty" thesis in a study of public housing residents in Hong Kong. For a discussion of public housing densities in Hong Kong and the inapplicability of the poverty thesis, see *Housing Provision in Metropolitan Hong Kong* (Hong Kong: Center of Asian Studies, University of Hong Kong, 1973), pp. 35, 40, 78.

16. Meehan, *Public Housing Policy*, p. 136.

17. Ibid., pp. 177–179.

18. Roger Starr, "Which of the Poor Shall Live in Public Housing?" passim.

19. Low-rent public housing units are eagerly sought not only in the United States, but in other nations as well. A survey of low-income families in Hong Kong revealed that the lowest priced public housing units were the most popular alternative among housing choices, even among families who could afford a better grade of subsidized but more costly housing or better private housing. See Drakakis-Smith, *Housing Provision in Metropolitan Hong Kong*, p. 82. Muth estimates that public housing tenants acquire about four times more housing per dollar spent than they would be able to obtain in the private market. See Richard F. Muth, *Public Housing: an Economic Evaluation* (Washington, D.C.: American Enterprise Institute for Public Policy Research, 1973), p. 20.

20. *1974 HUD Statistical Yearbook* (Washington, D.C.: U.S. Government Printing Office), pp. 65–67, 72.

21. See *Sixth Annual Report on National Housing Goals.* Message From the President of the United States, 94th Congress, 1st Session, House Document No. 194–18, January 14, 1975 (Washington, D.C.: U.S. Government Printing Office, 1975), p. 24.

22. Anthony Downs, *Federal Housing Subsidies, How Are They Working?* (Lexington: D.C. Heath, 1973), p. 36. Downs incorrectly equates the benefit of untaxed implicit rental income with a subsidy, though he is correct in that the financial benefits

of this tax policy exceed direct housing subsidies given to low-income families, but only in the aggregate, not on a family-by-family basis.

23. Ibid., p. 68.

24. Henry J. Aaron, *Shelter and Subsidies: Who Benefits from Federal Housing Policies?* (Washington, D.C.: Brookings Institution, 1972), p. 126.

25. Robert K. Brown, *Public Housing in Action: The Record of Pittsburgh* (Pittsburgh: University of Pittsburgh Press, 1959), pp. 80–81.

26. Muth, *Public Housing: An Economic Evaluation*.

27. Meehan gives specific figures in St. Louis. See *Public Housing Policy*, pp. 62–64.

28. Heilbrun, *Urban Economics and Public Policy*, p. 271.

29. *Housing in the Seventies. A Report of the National Housing Policy Review*. U.S. Department of Housing and Urban Development (Washington, D.C.: U.S. Government Printing Office, 1974), pp. 87–91, 124.

30. Robert C. Weaver, "Housing Allowances," *Land Economics* 51, No. 3 (August 1975), p. 254.

31. Lawrence M. Friedman, *Government and Slum Housing: A Century of Frustration* (Chicago: Rand McNally, 1968).

32. Leonard Freedman, *Public Housing: The Politics of Poverty* (New York: Holt, Rinehart and Winston, 1969).

33. Nathaniel S. Keith, *Politics and the Housing Crisis Since 1930* (New York: Universe Books, 1973).

34. Ibid., p. 12.

35. Aaron, *Shelter and Subsidies*, p. 112.

36. Albert A. Walsh, "Is Public Housing Headed for a Fiscal Crisis?" *Journal of Housing* 26, No. 2, February 1969, pp. 64–71.

37. Frank de Leeuw, *Operating Costs in Public Housing: A Financial Crisis* (Washington, D.C.: Urban Institute, 1969).

38. See "Myths/Realities of Public Housing," *Journal of Housing*, April 1973, p. 185. For a case study of the effects of the Brooke amendments on the Norfolk public housing program see "Money Cuts, New Rules—Hard Times for Public Housing," *U.S. News & World Report*, 26 March 1973, pp. 87–88.

39. HUD now uses a new performance funding system developed by the Urban Institute to dispense operating costs subsidies. This formula is to represent the operations of a prototype well-managed project and utilizes 24 measures of performance, all but five of which are subjective measures of tenant, management, employee, and official HUD satisfaction with the LHA. For a review and critique of the new performance funding system see *Operating Subsidies for Public Housing* (Boston: Citizens Housing and Planning Association of Metropolitan Boston, 1975).

40. *1974 HUD Statistical Yearbook*, p. 101.

41. See Richard S. Sterne, James E. Phillips, and Alvin Rabushka, *The Urban Elderly Poor: Racial and Bureaucratic Conflict* (Lexington: D.C. Heath, 1974), pp. 7–8.

42. Two other authors also advocate that local housing agencies examine the various dimensions of tenant satisfaction to assist in the provision of efficient housing services. They find that satisfaction with management is the most important factor in explaining overall tenant satisfaction, followed by satisfaction with neighboring and neighborhood services and, finally, maintenance. Understanding tenant preferences is a means to insure that the decision makers in the public housing delivery system *do not* "substitute their own biases for the preferences of the prospective consumers." See Roger S. Ahlbrandt, Jr. and Paul C. Brophy, "Increasing Efficiency in the Delivery of Federally Assisted Housing Services Through an Understanding of Tenant Preferences," in Gordon Tullock (ed.), *Frontiers of Economics* (Blacksburg: Center for Study of Public Choice, Virginia Polytechnic Institute and State University, 1976), pp. 123–137.

Chapter 3

1. A study of the Model Cities Neighborhood Area in Rochester, New York, conducted between 1971 and 1973, ascertained that elderly poor inner-city residents do not perceive themselves to be in great need of extensive social services. See Richard S. Sterne, James E. Phillips, and Alvin Rabushka, *The Urban Elderly Poor: Racial and Bureaucratic Conflict* (Lexington: D.C. Heath, 1974).

2. Other scholars have also found that poor urban residents do not project a substantially unfavorable image on public housing. Indeed, despite the characteristics of the massive structures that most residents live in, public housing in New York is regarded quite positively. See George S. Sternlieb and Bernard P. Indik, *The Ecology of Welfare: Housing and the Welfare Crisis in New York City* (New Brunswick: Transaction Books, 1973), p. 73.

Chapter 4

1. See Martha Derthick, *Uncontrollable Spending for Social Services Grants* (Washington, D.C.: Brookings Institution, 1975), for a detailed study of these matching funds for social services grants.

2. Eugene Meehan tells a similar story about the St. Louis Housing Authority, accusing it of being too willing to experiment with a variety of social remedies. A resident staff sociologist position became, in 1957, a community services section, which in turn was upgraded to a Division of Human Resources in 1963. The Missouri Welfare Division obtained federal support for an enormous welfare office in the city, using the projects as justification. Washington University spent a $750,000-grant interviewing tenants, and the litany of other social service-related efforts, research projects, training programs, day-care centers, etc., ran into additional millions. Despite these efforts, the public housing program steadily deteriorated physically, financially, and in public esteem. See

Public Housing Policy. Convention Versus Realty (New Brunswick: Center for Urban Policy Research, 1975), pp. 133–134. What began as a straightforward program in developing and operating apartments for low-income families in the 1930s was transformed, better yet subverted, in the 1950s and 1960s into a division of welfare conceptualized to ameliorate social problems. We share Meehan's critique of this transformation.

3. The Rochester *Times-Union* reports a similar incident on 8 July 1975. The Director of the Rochester Housing Authority had requested $526,043 from the state in federal funds, which would have been used to establish a 24-man around-the-clock RHA security force, but the State Division of Criminal Justice, which administers the federal funds, rejected the application stating that "The rate of incidence of major crimes within the various housing projects is not significant enough to warrant the allocation of federal funds." The RHA has hired, on its own, armed private guards to patrol its 2,600 low-income housing units and expects to pay $80,000 to $85,000 a year for this private armed security force. In addition to the tenants' need for additional security and safety, the RHA has spent up to $159,000 in one year on work directly connected with vandalism.

Thus despite the 1974 Housing and Community Development Act's specific recommendation that LHAs make provision for increased tenant security, this book and this accompanying footnote document two clear cases of the federal government saying one thing and doing another. In the former case in Wilmington, HUD regional officials vetoed the expenditure; in Rochester, the state authority said no on the use of federal funds.

Chapter 5

1. In this light, we are fascinated that HUD and the Ford Foundation have jointly announced a $21 million program to carry out tenant management experiments in Jersey City, Louisville, New Orleans, Rochester (New York), New Haven, and Oklahoma City in seven public housing projects encompassing 19,000 residents. This program is modeled on a Ford-sponsored pilot project in St. Louis in which a tenant management corporation reportedly helped reduce such public housing programs as vandalism, high vacancy rates, and rent delinquencies. See *San Francisco Examiner and Chronicle*, 19 December 1976, p. 24. This report is especially interesting in light of Meehan's claim that a previous effort to form tenant committees was soon disbanded for lack of interest and activity. See *Public Housing Policy. Convention Versus Reality* (New Brunswick: Center for Urban Policy Research, 1975), p. 134.

The five stated goals of HUD's Tenant Management Demonstration Program include more efficient management, less social delinquency, more job opportunities, heightened community spirit, and an overall sense of resident involvement. We suspect, though, that effective tenant management really represents the efforts of middle-class organizers who act and advocate on behalf of the tenants. See Richard S. Sterne et al., *The Urban Elderly Poor* (Lexington: D.C. Heath, 1974), Chapter 7, for an illustration of this argument.

2. For a comprehensive review of the literature and debate on multiproblem families see Richard S. Scobie, *Problem Tenants in Public Housing. Who, Where, and Why are they?* (New York: Praeger, 1975), Chapter 2.

3. See "Applicant Prediction Model and Program Model for Excessive Cost Families," September 28, 1973, pp. 16–23 in *Resident Referral Transfer Document Draft, Vol. II* (Wilmington Housing Authority, May 1975).

4. Using the evidence of Boston's public housing tenants, Scobie *(Problem Tenants in Public Housing)* rejects the notion that it is possible to reduce conflict and produce a relatively problem-free residential area by selecting out multiproblem tenants. See especially page 75. Thus the Wilmington experience was not unique.

5. For an excellent exposition of the difficulties encountered in implementing a federal program to provide jobs to minority group members see Aaron Wildavsky and Jeffrey L. Pressman, *Implementation* (Berkeley: University of California Press, 1973). For a more general discussion on the failure of social services to systematically reduce dependency or otherwise fundamentally change the lives of their recipients, see Joel Fischer, "Is Casework Effective? A Review," *Social Work* (January 1973) and *Social Services: Do They Help Welfare Recipients Achieve Self-Support or Reduced Dependency?*, Report to the Congress by the Comptroller General of the United States (June 1973).

6. Interview with the Deputy Director of Resident Services, Wilmington Housing Authority, 18 June 1975.

Chapter 6

1. See Robert Notte, "The Public Housing Program in Newark: Federal Policies and the Rent Strike," in Frederic M. Vogelsang (ed.), *Public Housing Management in the Seventies* (Washington, D.C.: National Association of Housing and Redevelopment Officials, 1974), p. 36.

2. *Appendix to the Budget for Fiscal Year 1976.* Department of Housing and Urban Development (Washington, D.C.: U.S. Government Printing Office, 1975), pp. 469–470.

3. See Robert Sadacca et al., *Management Performance in Public Housing* (Washington, D.C.: Urban Institute, 1974).

INDEX